MIKE KLEIN

Moundville

Small Villages - W. Jeff 850/900 - 1050

Simple Chiefdoms, Single Mound sites M'ville I 1050-1250

Complex Chiefdom, " II 1250 -1450
Moundville at the

Center
Add'l Single Mound " III 1450-1550 + Peak
centers/ adds

Villages, no Pratohist 1550 - 1700
regional ranking
Moundville abandoned

Moundville's Economy

Paul D. Welch

A Dan Josselyn Memorial Publication

THE UNIVERSITY OF ALABAMA PRESS

TUSCALOOSA AND LONDON

The paper on which this book is printed meets the minimum
requirements of American National Standard for Information
Science-Permanence of Paper for Printed Library Materials, ANSI
A39.48-1984.

Library of Congress Cataloging-in-Publication Data

Welch, Paul D., 1955–
    Moundville's economy / Paul D. Welch.
        p.   cm.
    "A Dan Josselyn memorial publication."
    Includes bibliographical references.
    ISBN 0-8173-0512-2 (alk. paper)
    1. Mississippian culture—Alabama.   2. Mound State
        Monument (Ala.)
    3. Indians of North America—Alabama—Economic conditions.
    4. Indians of North America—Alabama—Antiquities.   I. Title.
E99.M6815W45   1991
330.9761'4301—dc20   90-34220

British Library Cataloguing-in-Publication Data available

Contents

Figures and Tables

Tables

Acknowledgments

Much of the information in this book comes from the works of a group of scholars who have collaborated on Moundville research for over a decade. In addition to citing the various members of the group at the appropriate places in the text, I am pleased to state that the contributions of Christopher Peebles (the founder of the group), Vincas Steponaitis, and Margaret Scarry are greater than textual citation alone can convey. Their behind-the-scene ideas, support, and intelligent criticism were at least as vital to this study as their published research. I am grateful for their assistance and friendship.

Data from the 1983 excavations at the White site come from work supported by the National Science Foundation under Grant No. BNS-8305514 and by the H. H. Rackham School of Graduate Studies at the University of Michigan. Any opinions, findings, and conclusions or recommendations expressed in this material are those of the author and do not necessarily reflect the views of either institution.

I also wish to thank Stephen Kowalewski and an anonymous reviewer for the University of Alabama Press. Their comments were thoughtful, thorough, and constructive. They are not responsible, however, for any errors, interpretations, or lacunae that appear herein; those are properties of the author.

Moundville's Economy

1 Introduction

This study combines archaeological site catchment and locational data; stylistic, technological, and functional analysis of artifacts; and analysis of botanical and faunal remains in an effort to reconstruct the economy of a prehistoric chiefdom. There are several reasons for undertaking this study, beyond merely adding to our knowledge of past lifeways. Among students of cultural evolution there is widespread agreement that the chiefdom is the form of sociocultural organization from which the first states evolved (e.g., Sanders and Price 1968; Flannery 1972; Service 1975; Wright 1977, 1984; Carneiro 1981). The origin of the state being a persistent focus of research in the social sciences, much of the attention focused on chiefdoms has concerned the way(s) chiefdoms may be transformed into states. On the other hand, archaeological and ethnohistorical records from Polynesia, the southeastern United States, and Europe during the Bronze and Iron Ages make it clear that the chiefdom level of sociocultural integration may be the dominant form of political organization in a region for hundreds or even thousands of years, with no autochthonous evolution of states. Individual chiefdoms come and go on a time scale of a few hundred years at most, but the region as a whole continues to be characterized by this form of polity. Chiefdoms, thus, are of interest not only because they evolved into states, but also because much more frequently they did not (see Drennan and Uribe 1987; Earle 1987, 1989). The persistence of

1

this form of sociocultural integration is itself a matter of interest.

Researchers use the term *chiefdom* to denote nonstate societies with ascriptive hierarchical ranking. A brief review of the history of the term, as well as a more specific definition, is presented in chapter two. That chapter also documents the fact that while there is consensus on the form of political organization denoted by the term, there is disagreement about the economic organization of such polities. By *economic organization,* I mean the pattern(s) of production, distribution, and consumption of various sorts of goods. From an anthropological perspective, this disagreement is surprising. As a nonmarket society, the economy of a chiefdom is not a realm of relationships and interactions separable from other aspects of social interaction. This is the basic tenet of the "substantive" school of economic thought (see Polanyi 1957a, 1957b; Fusfeld 1957; Dalton 1961; Firth 1965; Forde and Douglas 1967; Sahlins 1972). As Dalton (1961, 21) put it, economic relations are the manifestations of social relations. Since chiefdoms, to use Service's (1971, 145) phrase, are characterized by "pervasive inequality of persons and groups," material transactions between such persons or groups are inherently as much political as economic in nature. Therefore, the current situation in anthropology is that there is some consensus about the political structure of chiefdoms but disagreement over the structure of their political economies, despite the fact that the political economy is a material manifestation of political relations.

The debate over the structure of chiefdom economy has revealed that the ethnographic and ethnohistorical record contains considerable ambiguity about actual transactions in chiefdoms. Hawaiian chiefdoms, for example, have been cited as supporting contradictory economic models. Ambiguity can stem from the naive imposition of Western concepts on non-Western social settings, acceptance by the observer of chiefly ideology as an accurate representation of the actual economy, the short time span and narrow geographic basis of observations, and probably other factors as well. Since chiefdom societies can no longer be observed firsthand, the only new evidence to bring to bear on the issue is archaeological. This, however, is easier said than done.

For archaeological data to be of help in determining how chiefdom economies were structured, the data must meet certain criteria. First, it must be shown that the data derive from a society that was organized as a chiefdom. This demonstration must be made on the basis of noneconomic criteria, in order to avoid logical circularity. Second, the archaeological data should be as direct as possible. Archaeological data are never fully direct evidence of past behavior but are, rather, by-products of, or patterned to some extent by, past behavior. However, some data are less indirect than others: the identification of preserved agricultural field patterns and the recovery of macroscopic remains of domesticated plants, for example, provide more direct evidence of an agricultural economy than does an association of settlements with fertile soils. A third criterion that must be met is that the archaeologist must be able to determine what social context the data provide information about. For example, it is important to know whether a refuse deposit contains refuse from a chiefly residence or debris from a low-ranking household. A fourth criterion is related to this point: data should be gathered from as many distinct social contexts as possible. Since the controversy over chiefdom economies concerns the pattern of movement of goods between settlements as well as between levels in the social hierarchy, minimally there should be data from each type of settlement in the settlement system.

Few sets of archaeological data meet these criteria. In

effect, what is required is multidisciplinary analysis of data from multiple sites, where chronology and political geography are understood, and where there is a sound, noneconomic basis for inferring the form of political organization. Such sets of data are most likely to be generated when researchers with complementary interests and skills work under the guidance of an integrated research design. Just such a group of scholars has studied the Mississippian chiefdom centered at Moundville, Alabama. Information they have furnished, in combination with data from my own fieldwork, makes the Moundville case one of the few sets of archaeological data that meet the criteria outlined above. The archaeological record of the Moundville chiefdom is examined to provide, as fully as possible, answers to the classic questions of political economy: who produces what for whom, and how is it transferred from producers to consumers? In order to focus these questions more sharply, and to cast them in terms appropriate to chiefdom economies in particular, the debate over the structure of chiefdom economies is reviewed and those models extant in the literature are outlined. The contrasts between the models serve as the source of the questions explicitly posed of the archaeological data. A model of the structure of the prehistoric Moundville economy is then built from the answers to these questions, and the logical implications of this structural model are explored.

This is essentially a case study. It is not designed to provide an indication about how all chiefdom economies were structured. Rather, the goal is to determine how one particular chiefdom was organized. With this information in hand, further issues can then be addressed, such as determining what factors might have led to instability and collapse of this economy. This study is merely one step toward the goal stated at the opening of this chapter, namely, elucidating the causes of persistence or transformation of chiefdoms.

The study is organized as follows. The controversy over chiefdom economies is reviewed in chapter two. Alternative models are described and their contrasting features made explicit. Chapter three introduces the archaeology of the Moundville chiefdom and describes the strengths and weaknesses of the extant data. The excavations I directed to complement these data are also described. Subsistence data are analyzed in chapter four, including catchment analysis and analysis of faunal and botanical remains from the Moundville paramount center and a subsidiary site. The production and distribution of craft items are examined in chapter five. The sixth chapter summarizes the results of the study and addresses two further issues: the external economic relations of the Moundville chiefdom and the dynamic behavior of the Moundville economy.

2 Theoretical Background

Introduction

The term *chiefdom* came to have a technical meaning in anthropology during the 1950s. Carneiro (1981) has recently reviewed this process, and interested readers are referred to his article for details. In brief, Oberg (1955) and Steward and Faron (1959) first used the term in a defined sense, to denote ranked, multivillage polities headed by a paramount chief. It was Elman Service, however, who firmly established the term in our lexicon when he used it to denote one of the four classificatory/evolutionary stages in his highly influential *Primitive Social Organization* (1971 [1st ed. 1962]). Service's definition of a chiefdom is too protracted to quote in its entirety, but the main points are present in the following passage:

> A chiefdom occupies a level of social integration which transcends tribal society in two important respects. First, a chiefdom is usually a denser society than is a tribe, a gain made possible by greater productivity. But second, and more indicative of the evolutionary stage, the society is also more complex and more organized, being particularly distinguished from tribes by the presence of centers which coordinate economic, social, and religious activities. . . . The increased productivity and greater population density of chiefdoms are not necessarily due to any particular technological development,

although in some instances it is apparent that such development did take place. More frequently, and in all cases importantly, the rise of chiefdoms seems to have been related to a total environmental situation which was selective for specialization in production and redistribution of produce from a controlling center. . . . [S]pecialization and redistribution are [not] merely adjunctive to a few particular endeavors, but continuously characterize a large part of the activity of the society. Chiefdoms are *redistributional societies* with a permanent central agency of coordination. (Service 1971, 133–34, emphasis in original)

Service argued that redistribution was the cause for the evolution of chiefdoms and was the way that chiefdom economies functioned. Other researchers have called into question the nature or even presence of redistribution in prestate societies. Service's chiefdom concept has proved so useful in anthropology, however, that even those who disagree with the importance of redistribution continue to use the term *chiefdom* for societies with social, political, and religious characteristics more or less as outlined by Service (e.g., Taylor 1975; Peebles and Kus 1977; Earle 1977, 1978, 1987, 1989; Steponaitis 1978; Carneiro 1981; Drennan and Uribe 1987). I follow this practice by accepting Wright's (1977, 381; 1984) definition of a chiefdom as a sociocultural formation with a decision-making hierarchy lacking internal differentiation and having no more that two to three levels above the level of local production and local social process. While Wright went on to suggest a "dominant strategy" for the economy of such an entity, economic structure is not a component of, nor entailed by, the definition. This leaves the issue of economic structure as a question that can be answered empirically. Contrasting models of chiefdom economy, including redistribution, are reviewed in this chapter.

Redistribution

In addition to reviewing the history of the chiefdom concept, Carneiro (1981, 58–63) traces the intellectual route by which redistribution came to be a fundamental component of Service's chiefdom definition. In brief, Carneiro attributes the origin of the redistribution concept to Thurnwald (1932). Polanyi (1957b) elaborated on the concept, and Sahlins (1958, xi), much influenced by Polanyi, made it an important feature of his analysis of Polynesian societies: "Everywhere in Polynesia, the chief is the agent of general, tribal-wide distribution. The chief derives prestige from his generosity. In turn, his prestige permits him to exercise control over social processes, such as production, upon which his functions of distribution rest. Consequently, the greater the productivity, the greater the distributive activities of the chief, and the greater his powers." Because Service was "strongly influenced" by Sahlins's study, Carneiro contends, redistribution was given central importance in Service's definition of the chiefdom. Indeed, Service (1971, 134) cited Sahlins's study as an example of the role of redistribution in Polynesian chiefdoms.

There is, however, another obvious reason that redistribution has been seen as a basic feature of chiefdoms. Many ethnographies and ethnohistories of chiefdom societies describe a flow of goods that is suggestive of redistribution. For example, we find the following statements about the Bemba of southeastern Africa, the Polynesian chiefdom of Moala, and the Natchez of the southeastern United States, respectively:

> The whole institution of the [sacred kitchen of the chief] illustrates to my mind that close association between authority and the power to distribute provisions on which the tribal organization depends. The chief owns the food and receives tribute, and the chief provides for his sub-

jects and distributes cooked food to them. (Richards 1961, 150)

. . . the chief mobilized not only the labor of his own large household but likewise that of his subordinate chiefs and their kin. Thus, the paramount would collect a significant amount of the surplus production of the community and redistribute it in the general welfare. In this way he achieved prestige and bolstered his political status. Moreover, in contracting to subsidize the general welfare, his activities stimulated the general productivity. (Sahlins 1962, 294)

Once in the summer, toward the end of July, the people gather by order of the great chief to be present at a grand feast which he gives them. This festival lasts for three days and three nights, and each one contributes what he can to furnish it; some bring game, others fish, etc. (Le Petit, quoted in Swanton 1911, 122)

For Service, however, redistribution did not mean merely the movement of goods in to the chief and then back out again. Rather, redistribution was a means of coordinating specialized producers. The chiefdom was seen as being composed of productive units, be they villages or districts, each of which specialized in producing a specific set of goods. None of the productive units was self-sufficient, and redistribution was the mechanism by which each of the units received those essential goods that they did not themselves produce. Each unit passed a substantial amount of their products to a central location, where the chief recombined the varied products and parceled them out so that each unit received the complete suite of the goods they needed.

Redistribution, Service argued (1971, 136; 1975, 75–78), would typically arise in settings of sedentary communities in a region of geographically diversified resources. Several other possibilities were noted, such as redistribution coordinating diversified, specialized producers in a geographically homogeneous environment (Service 1975, 77, footnote 5), and allocation of the products resulting from communal but complexly specialized, centrally directed labor (1971, 136–37). Little space was devoted to describing these alternatives, and Service (especially 1975, 75–78) made it clear that he considered them informative but atypical.

In its classic sense, then, redistribution is the centrally directed reallocation of necessary goods to non-self-suf-

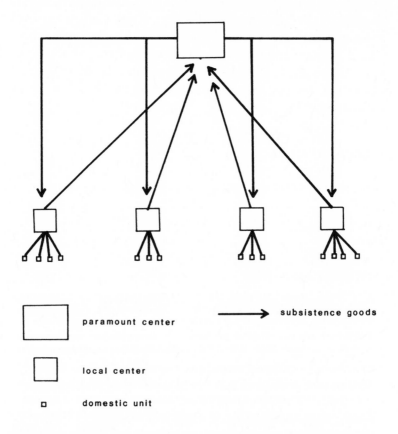

▭ paramount center	⟶ subsistence goods
▢ local center	
▫ domestic unit	

Figure 2.1 Schematic Diagram of the Classic Redistribution Model

ficient, specialized producers, typically in a geographically diversified setting. This pattern of movement of goods is presented in schematic form in figure 2.1. The figure depicts a chiefdom with a paramount center and four districts each with a local center. A portion of the produce of each domestic unit is passed to the local center and thence to the paramount center. There the products are recombined and sent to the local centers for distribution to the producers. The goods being moved are labeled "subsistence goods," but in addition to foodstuffs, they may include any items necessary for the physical reproduction of society, such as agricultural and hunting implements, cooking utensils, and winter clothing. Movements of items of primarily social or symbolic value, such as sumptuary goods, are not shown in figure 2.1, since Service did not discuss the production of these goods.

Alternative Models

The redistribution model was widely accepted as *the* economic structure of chiefdoms until the mid-1970s (see, for example, Fried 1967, 116–18). Perhaps the first challenge to this assumption was made by Taylor (1975). In her comparative study of east and central African polities, she found that:

> The middle-range hierarchical societies of the present sample are not typically differentiated and redistributive societies as delineated in the . . . "chiefdom" model. . . . In all the societies of this sample, including most of the centrally organized ones, local groups tend to be very largely self-sufficient, and to provide most or all of their own material needs. Chieftaincy in this sample is not typically characterized by the central coordination of the specialized activities of unlike parts of the whole. (Taylor 1975, 35–36)

Curiously, Taylor's study was not generally cited in the literature on chiefdoms until the 1980s.

The next two studies to take issue with the redistribution concept were both based on Hawaiian data and appeared in 1977. Earle (1977, 1978) showed that community territories in Hawaii were structured so as to maximize environmental diversity within the territory and minimize differences between territories. This, together with the traditional community social organization, permitted each community to be self-sufficient. The second study, by Kus (Peebles and Kus 1977), marshaled ethnohistorical evidence to show that, while substantial quantities of food and craft items were provided to the paramount chief by each community, these goods were not redistributed throughout the chiefdom. Rather, they were used almost exclusively to support the paramount, his court, and his army. Both of these studies concluded that the redistribution model was inaccurate, at least for Hawaii. This conclusion was particularly significant because Hawaiian chiefdoms were among the most complex known and were widely taken as paradigmatic examples of the chiefdom construct.

Since 1977, other studies have taken issue with the presumed association of chiefdom political structure and redistributional economy. Helms's (1979) analysis of ethnohistorical records from Panama showed that area to have been occupied by a network of chiefdoms at the time of Spanish contact. The ethnohistorical records, however, contain no mention of redistribution-like activities (Helms 1979, 14–15). Similarly, Steponaitis's (1978, 421–26) review of the relevant ethnohistoric information revealed that redistribution was not the basis of the political economy in the Society Islands (Tahiti) or among the Natchez of the southeastern United States. And from their comparative analysis of New World prestate societies, Feinman and Neitzel (1984, 56) concluded:

. . . redistribution is clearly not the central function of leadership in sedentary prestate societies. Weak leaders only occasionally redistribute; and although the importance of redistribution increases among strong leaders, this activity is not shared by all of them. . . . It should be noted that [here], "redistribution" refers to a diverse set of activities. If by "redistribution" one implies merely the distribution of food and other goods by leaders [i.e., classic redistribution], then the relative importance of this task is diminished further.

Studies critical of the redistribution model for chiefdoms proliferated in the 1980s (see Earle 1987, 291–98, for a review).

From these studies, it has become clear that the classic redistribution model does not accurately describe the structure of some, perhaps most, chiefdom economies. As noted above, Service never claimed that *all* chiefdoms were redistributional, but he did state that redistribution was the typical economic structure. Moreover, some of the societies he cited as examples of redistributional economies are among those that other researchers have argued were not redistributional. Much of the controversy is undoubtedly due to ambiguity in the ethnographic and ethnohistoric record. For example, I quote above a passage from Richards (1961) that purports to show that redistribution was important among the Bemba. In fact, however, Bemba chiefs distributed food primarily to "tribute workers, courtiers, executive officials, or visiting councillors on tribal business" (Richards 1961, 147), rather than to economically diversified outlying communities. The critiques of the redistribution concept have made it clear that an accurate understanding of the economic structure of chiefdoms must be based on detailed quantitative information about the loci of production and use or consumption of goods, combined with information about the mode of distribution. Since such information is not generally available in ethnographic and ethnohistoric records, the issue must be resolved with archaeological data.

In addition to casting doubt on the ubiquity or presence of redistribution in chiefdoms, the studies cited above (plus others) proposed alternative models of chiefdom economy. Unlike the redistribution model, these models deal not only with the production and distribution of craft items and prestige goods but also with food and utilitarian items.

The reassessments of ethnography and ethnohistory that cast out redistribution (e.g., Taylor 1975; Peebles and Kus 1977; Earle 1977, 1978, 1987) concur in finding that local units in a chiefdom are largely or wholly self-sufficient in average years. Exchanges between units were based on reciprocity and did not involve the administrative hierarchy (Peebles and Kus 1977, 424–25; Earle 1977, 224–25). Chiefs did receive tribute of foodstuffs (Taylor 1975, 37–39; Peebles and Kus 1977, 425–26; Earle 1978, 187–90) or labor to produce food for the chief's use (Helms 1979, 14). Figure 2.2 schematically diagrams these flows of subsistence goods. Following Earle (1977, 215–16; cf. Dalton 1961), I refer to this economic model as mobilization.

One aspect of the economic model outlined by Earle and Peebles and Kus is not shown in figure 2.2, specifically, buffering against environmental fluctuation. The most general buffering mechanism in chiefdoms is the maintenance of large stores of food by the chief, which are used to support individuals in need (Taylor 1975, 38; Peebles and Kus 1977, 430–31; Helms 1979, 11). In times of subsistence shortfalls that exceed the buffering capacity of the chiefly stores, chiefs may also exploit external political connections to obtain "disaster relief" (e.g., Sahlins 1962, 369; Spillius 1957). As a component of the mobilization model, buffering would be shown in figure 2.2 as movement of subsistence goods from the paramount center to individual domestic units. Buffering (in the form of chiefly storage) was also a component of the redistribution model (Service 1971, 139). This episodic movement of subsistence goods has been left out of figures 2.1 and 2.2 in order to make clear the contrasts between these two diagrams.

Just as there are models of the movement of subsistence goods, there are models of the production and distribution of craft items. Two contrasting models have been articulated by Wright (1977, 1984; see also Peebles

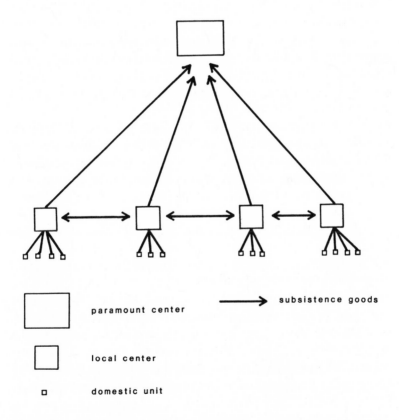

Figure 2.2 Schematic Diagram of the Mobilization Model

and Kus 1977) and by Frankenstein and Rowlands (1978). Before reviewing these models, a short discussion of nomenclature is necessary. Since these models are referred to repeatedly in this study, it is convenient to have short, simple names for them. Names for these models are not yet established in the literature, and the most obvious candidate terms do not intrinsically convey the significant distinctions between the two models. Frankenstein and Rowlands (1978) refer to their model as a *prestige goods economy*. Rather than proliferate terms, I follow their lead; however, it must be kept in mind that *prestige goods economy* specifically designates the Frankenstein and Rowlands model and not just any model of the prestige goods sector of an economy. Wright (1984) uses the term *tributary economy* in connection with his model of Hawaiian political economy. Though he did not use the term in a definitional sense, I adopt *tributary* as a label for the model he presented. Though it has the disadvantage of sounding as if it denotes the economy of a tributary polity, which is not intended, it has the advantage of focusing attention on the movement of tribute goods.

The tributary model outlined by Wright (1977, 381–82; 1984) is explicitly a reexpression of Peebles and Kus's (1977) interpretation of Hawaiian economic structure. Aside from presenting the model in more abstract terms, it differs from the Peebles and Kus formulation only in focusing on the direct and, particularly, the indirect feedback mechanisms inherent in the model. Wright (1984) describes the model with admirable clarity: "[While] food and goods are extracted as tribute from producers, actual distribution is characteristically to lesser figures within the chiefdom, rather than to the whole populace, and the redistributed items are often goods made by specialists, either part-time specialists locally supported by commoner production or full-time specialists supported by chiefs using some of the tribute extracted from producers."

The tributary model of production and distribution of craft items is shown in figure 2.3. The pattern is superficially similar to that shown in figure 2.1, but in addition to dealing with different kinds of goods, this pattern differs in three ways from figure 2.1. First, the four districts do not produce mutually exclusive sets of

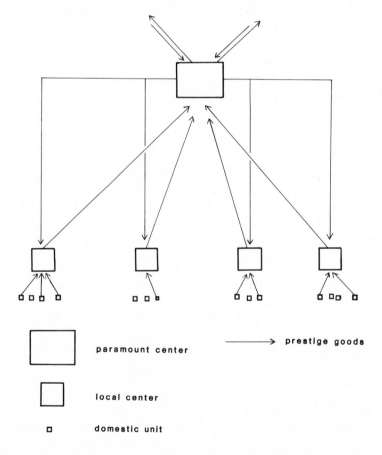

Figure 2.3 Schematic Diagram of the Tributary Model

craft items. Second, all four local centers receive from the paramount the same set of craft items, and this set includes only a subset of the range of items available to the paramount either from tribute or from exchange with external polities. The third difference between this pattern and that shown in figure 2.1 is that none of the items distributed by the paramount to the local centers reaches the level of the domestic units. Instead, all the distributed craft items are kept by the local nobility.

Unlike the models described above, the prestige goods model of Frankenstein and Rowlands (1978) is not presented as an ethnographic or ethnohistoric case study. It is, rather, presented as a logical construct based on the observation that political power is often associated with control over access to foreign goods that have been assigned high status:

> The specific economic characteristics of a prestige goods system are dominated by the political advantage gained through exercising control over access to resources that can only be obtained through external trade. However, these are not resources required for general material well-being or for the manufacture of tools and other utilitarian items. Instead, emphasis is placed on controlling the acquisition of wealth objects needed in social transactions, and the payment of social debts. . . . The use of domestic wealth objects will be devalued and restricted to relatively minor social transactions, and a sphere of foreign wealth objects will be formalised to take their place. . . . The chief's control over external trade in wealth objects is absolute so that he alone obtains commodities from a foreign source which he can then redistribute in the form of status insignia, funerary goods, bridewealth, etc. . . . This serves to emphasise the importance of political control over the domestic resources that form the source of exchangeable wealth for external trade. Under these conditions, there will be a tendency to select for those resources that are not found to be dis-

tributed evenly and can therefore be more easily controlled. (Frankenstein and Rowlands 1978, 76–77)

This model is diagrammed in figure 2.4. Note that locally produced crafts passed to the paramount as tribute
do not circulate within the chiefdom, and that only a
subset of the nonlocal prestige goods available to the
paramount are distributed to the local nobility.

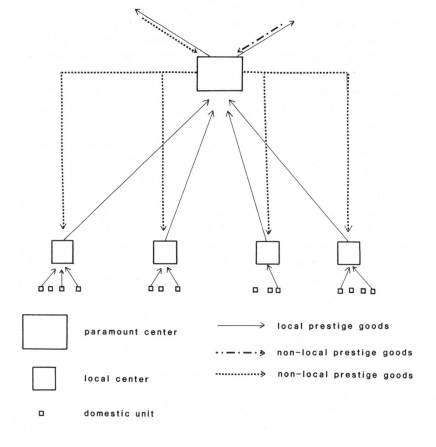

Figure 2.4 Schematic Diagram of the Prestige Goods Model

Conclusion

The models diagrammed in figures 2.1 through 2.4 are, of course, not the only conceivable models. There are many ways to draw arrows between the boxes that represent levels of the settlement hierarchy. For example, the patterns do not have to be symmetric; one local center might stand out in contrast to the others, or the nature of tribute flows and redistributed goods might vary with distance from the local center to the paramount site (cf. Steponaitis 1978, 444–49). Furthermore, each of the diagrams represents only one sector of a functioning economy, either the prestige goods sector or the subsistence sector. These partial models can be combined in four discrete ways—many more if the combinations are mixed or asymmetric. Actually, both Wright (1977, 1984) and Frankenstein and Rowlands (1978) argue that their models of prestige goods production and distribution are associated with subsistence economies of the mobilization type. Thus there are actually only three discrete models in the literature reviewed here: the classic redistribution, mobilization + tributary, and mobilization + prestige goods models. Incidentally, it should be clear that I do not intend these models as distinct modes of production in a Marxist sense, for the models only describe abstract patterns of production and distribution and do not deal with either the forces or means of production.

Despite the differences in their structure, each of these models focuses on roughly the same set of issues. Minimally, these issues include the following:

1. Are the settlements within a chiefdom self-sufficient in production of food and other necessary economic goods, or is there complementary specialization of the production of these goods?

2. If there is complementary specialization of production of necessary economic goods, how are the goods

distributed? Specifically, are the goods transferred by direct exchanges between producers and consumers, or is the distribution effected by a central manager (the chief)?

3. Is there mobilization of subsistence goods to support the elite?

4. Is there specialization of production of craft items? How are craft items distributed?

5. Is the mode of production and distribution of prestige goods different from that of utilitarian items?

6. How do nonlocal goods enter the chiefdom, and how are they distributed?

By obtaining answers to these questions from any particular chiefdom, we can determine which aspects of the economic models are accurate in that particular instance. The goal of such research, however, should not be to determine which model is the "real" economic structure of a chiefdom. These models are ideal types. Historical, contingent factors in specific past sociocultural formations can be expected to result in economies that differ from these ideal types. Moreover, the reason for constructing models is not to obtain a completely accurate representation of an actual economy. Models are logical constructs that have calculable properties given certain theoretical assumptions. To the extent that an actual economy conforms to a particular model, we would expect the properties of the model also to apply. By evaluating these expectations against actual economic data, we can determine whether our theoretical assumptions are in need of revision.

As logical constructs, the models discussed here have contrasting implications about the causes of stability and change in chiefdoms. For example, maintenance of the social hierarchy in a chiefdom with a mobilization + prestige goods economy is dependent upon continuing external exchange. In contrast, external exchange is not required for a classic redistributional economy. The models also differ in terms of whether economic stability would be perturbed by such factors as localized crop failure, geographically uneven demographic change within the chiefdom, and intentional manipulation by competitors for the paramountcy. To anticipate the results of the Moundville case study, the economy of the Moundville chiefdom differs sufficiently from each of the models discussed above so that the implications for the dynamics of the economy differ from the implications of each of the models.

3 The Test Case

The Moundville Chiefdom

The Mississippian chiefdom centered at Moundville, Alabama, during the eleventh to sixteenth centuries A.D., is archaeologically well known. An unusually large body of data on the chiefdom already exists, both in the literature and in museums. Previous analyses of some of these data document the society's organization as a complex chiefdom, as well as many aspects of settlement pattern, cultural history, economy, diet, etc. As a prehistoric polity, it has clear geographic boundaries, with archaeological components of the chiefdom clustered within 20 km of Moundville. Beyond this radius, the area was largely unpopulated. This allows us to distinguish between components of the chiefdom and the nearby polities that had some other political relation to this chiefdom. Since much of the extant information on the Moundville chiefdom is published in widely available sources, the following review will focus on the conclusions drawn by previous analyses rather than on details of data and analytic technique. Such details will be included, however, in the description of the new research that forms the core of this study.

Environmental Setting

Settlements of the Moundville chiefdom were located along a 40-km stretch of the floodplain of the Black War-

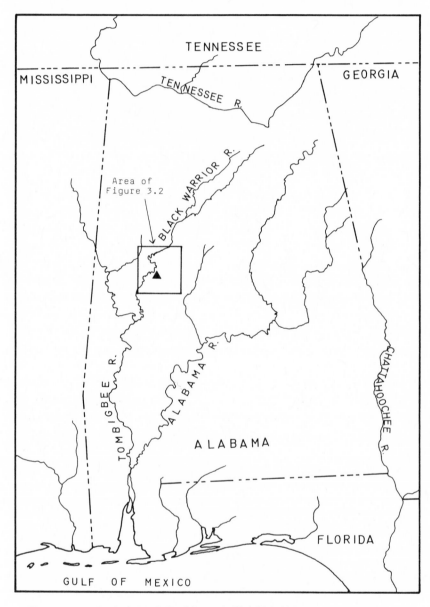

Figure 3.1 Location of the Moundville Chiefdom

rior River below Tuscaloosa, Alabama (see figure 3.1). Tuscaloosa is the location of the river's fall line, below which the river meanders in an alluvial valley 5 to 8 km wide. As Peebles (1978a, 388–93; 1978b, 43) has emphasized, this location provided members of the chiefdom

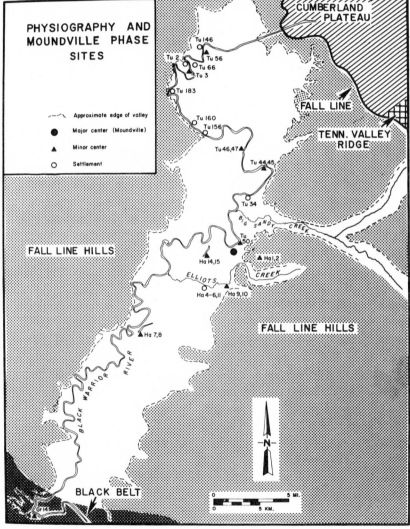

Figure 3.2 Physiography of the Moundville Area

*Numerous
Edges
attract
dw.*

with easy access to the oak-chestnut and mixed mesophytic forests in the Cumberland Plateau and Tennessee
Valley Ridge physiographic provinces, the prairies of
the Black Belt, the bottomland hardwoods of the
floodplain itself, and the oak-pine forest of the Fall Line
Hills (see figure 3.2). The floodplain forests surrounding settlements of the Moundville chiefdom were a rich
and complex interdigitation of stands of bald cypress
(Taxodium distichum) in permanently inundated soils;
sweetgum *(Liquidambar styraciflua),* holly *(Ilex* sp.),
and black gum *(Nyssa sylvatica)* in permanently wet
soils; large tracts of oaks *(Quercus* sp.) in seasonally wet
soils; and mixed hardwoods on natural levees and terrace edges (Scarry 1986). Along with fauna of the river
and its oxbow lakes, this rich floral assemblage and its
fauna provided moderate to high densities of all major
nonagricultural foodstuffs exploited by historic Indians
of the Southeast (Swanton 1946, 265–381).

The Black Warrior floodplain is also highly productive
for agriculture, using either prehistoric or modern technology. The most fertile soils (under early twentieth-
century management practices—see Peebles 1978a,
400–403) are loams, most of them easily tillable with
aboriginal technology. The frost-free growing season
exceeds 200 days nine years out of ten (Johnson 1981,
77; Edwards et al. 1939, 4). Precipitation during the
growing season averages 8 to 12 cm per month, though
during the summer, rainfall is unpredictable in location,
amount, intensity, and regularity. This variability can
be buffered, however, by planting in a variety of soils
and locations (cf. Chmurny 1973). For more discussion,
see the chapters on exploitation of specific resources.

History of Research

The extensive field research in the Moundville area
has been described in several publications (Peebles 1979,

1981; Bozeman 1982; Steponaitis 1983a, 1983b), so this review focuses on the nature of the extant data base, its strengths, and its weaknesses. The Moundville site itself (see figure 3.3) has been excavated sporadically for over

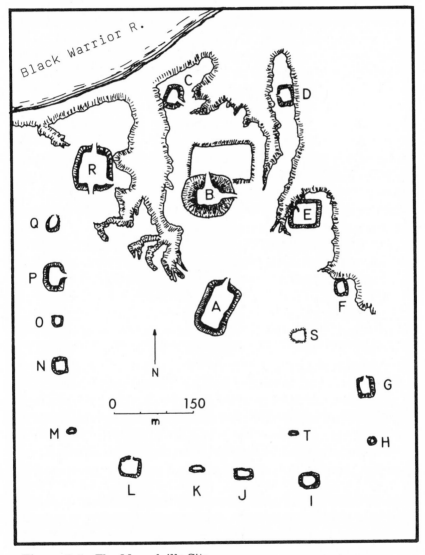

Figure 3.3 The Moundville Site

140 years (Peebles 1979, 1981; Steponaitis 1983a, 1983b). The bulk of our information about Moundville comes from the efforts of C. B. Moore (1905, 1907) and D. L. DeJarnette (see Wimberly 1956; Peebles 1979). Moore attacked all of the visible mounds and large parts of the site's high-status precincts. His reports and field notes almost exclusively provide information on mortuary associations. In contrast, DeJarnette's excavations focused on the nonmound area and provide information on nonmortuary aspects of the site. Excavations by DeJarnette and his successors at the University of Alabama have continued to the present, with the WPA labor crews of the 1930s being replaced in more recent times by field school students. These extensive excavations (roughly 5 ha) in general lacked tight stratigraphic control, and as sediments were rarely screened, artifact recovery was strongly biased toward complete, large, and unusual items.

The allure of the large, impressive Moundville site has not forestalled investigation of its environs. Moore (1905) tested half a dozen platform mounds on the Black Warrior floodplain between Tuscaloosa and Eutaw, Alabama, finding nothing to interest him. In the 1930s, the Alabama Museum of Natural History began compiling an archaeological site file. In addition to visiting the known Black Warrior floodplain sites, the museum also excavated cemetery areas at two single-mound sites near Moundville (DeJarnette and Peebles 1970; Jones and DeJarnette n.d.; DeJarnette, field notes on file at Mound State Monument). Aside from a few, very minor salvage expeditions and the excavation of some Protohistoric cemeteries not of concern here, the outlying sites received no further attention until the 1970s. At that time, many of the floodplain sites were revisited and small surface collections taken (Nielsen et al. 1973). Subsequently, John Walthall directed the intensive survey of a 6-km² section of floodplain and valley margin, as well as excavation of a small portion of a Late Woodland occupation (Walthall, field notes on file at Mound State Monument; Bozeman 1982, 157–59). This was followed by controlled surface collections and mound stratigraphy testing as part of Christopher Peebles's Moundville project (Bozeman 1982). Another section of the floodplain (4.45 km²) was intensively surveyed by Lawrence Alexander (1982) and small-scale excavations undertaken (Mistovich 1986, 1987). Furthermore, informal site surveys by both professional and avocational archaeologists have covered much of the remaining floodplain. The bluffs overlooking the floodplain, however, have received very little attention. We know that there are Late Woodland sites on the bluffs, but whether there are Mississippian sites there is not known. In short, we have good survey coverage of the floodplain near Moundville, but no coverage outside the floodplain and few excavation data from outside Moundville.

Current Status of Research at Moundville

Our current understanding of the Moundville chiefdom is largely the product of research conceived, directed, and executed by Christopher Peebles. It was he, in the late 1960s, who first attempted to organize the vast bulk of the excavation records from Moundville into a coherent account of the excavations and their results (see Peebles 1979; an earlier attempt by Douglas McKenzie [1964, 1965, 1966] was far less detailed). Having organized the excavation records, Peebles analyzed the Moundville mortuary program, demonstrating its conformity to the expectations for a complex chiefdom (Peebles 1971, 1972, 1974; Peebles and Kus 1977). This was followed by analyses of the location of settlements within the chiefdom by Peebles (1978a) and Steponaitis

(1978). These locational analyses ultimately had to be re-done as a result of information from the next phase of Moundville research (Bozeman 1982).

As one result of Peebles's analyses of the extant ar-chaeological data, several major gaps in the data became obvious. The most serious problem was the inability to make chronological distinctions within the temporal span of the Moundville chiefdom. This span was thought to be between 300 and 400 years (A.D. 1100–1200 to 1500–1550 [Peebles 1978c, 33]), which in retro-spect is an underestimate. To resolve this problem, Peebles proposed the construction of a ceramic chro-nology through seriation of vessels from grave lots, with the analysis to be performed by Vincas Steponaitis. Steponaitis's analysis (1980, 1983a) resulted in a tripar-tite division of the Moundville era—now seen as 500 years long—into Moundville I (A.D. 1050–1250), Moundville II (A.D. 1250–1400), and, not surprisingly, Moundville III (A.D. 1400–1550). Furthermore, "early" and "late" distinctions were made within these phases. Stratigraphic and chronometric support for this chro-nology was provided by deep stratigraphic excavations at Moundville directed by Margaret Scarry.

Scarry's excavations at Moundville were the second focus of Peebles's research project. The excavations were designed to provide the first systematically collected subsistence remains, using both fine-mesh waterscreen-ing and flotation (Scarry 1981a, 1981b; Michals 1981). A secondary goal of the excavations was to provide strat-igraphic and chronometric verification of Steponaitis's ceramic seriation. As a result of the nature of the depos-its sampled, most of Scarry's excavation data comes from the Moundville I phase. Scarry's data come from con-texts that are restricted sociologically as well as chrono-logically, for her excavations are located in precincts that appear to have encompassed something other than residences for commoners.

The third focus of Peebles's project was collection of

information about the chronology and size of outlying settlements. This was accomplished by mapping, controlled surface collection, and mound stratigraphy test excavation. These data were analyzed by Tandy Bozeman (1982), resulting in considerable revision of our picture of the Moundville settlement system. Briefly, we can now trace the development of the Moundville settlement system from small Late Woodland (A.D. 850 or 900 to 1050) villages, to four early Moundville I simple chiefdoms centered on single-mound sites. These communities were integrated into a complex chiefdom centered at Moundville in late Moundville I times. From the end of Moundville I to late Moundville III, Moundville remained the paramount site, while the locations of the outlying single-mound centers shifted within stable districts. Additional districts, and single-mound centers, were added to the south end of the chiefdom. This development is shown in figure 3.4. Throughout the Moundville I to late Moundville III span, there was only a small population resident at the single-mound sites, perhaps no more than a dozen households at each site. A much larger segment of the population, we suspect, resided in districts or neighborhoods of dispersed farmsteads and occasional hamlets, centered around the single-mound sites and Moundville. The number, density, and distribution (in both space and time) of farmsteads is not yet known; surveys demonstrate their presence but are not yet adequate for quantifying them (also note that farmsteads have not been depicted in figure 3.4). In late Moundville III times, population began to nucleate at some single-mound sites. In the following Protohistoric phase (A.D. 1550–1700, sometimes referred to as Moundville IV), the population of the valley was grouped into a set of villages whose mortuary remains show no evidence of intravillage or intervillage social ranking. By the beginning of this phase, the Moundville site apparently had been abandoned, and the complex chiefdom evidently had disintegrated.

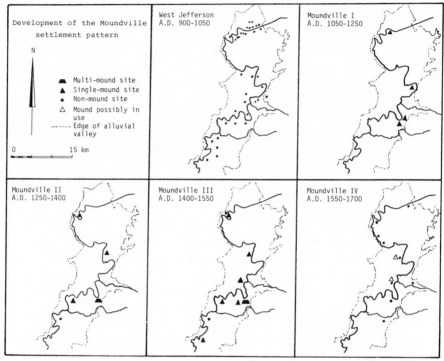

Figure 3.4 Development of the Moundville Settlement Pattern

Peebles's Moundville research project had additional goals and collaborators other than those already mentioned (see Schoeninger and Peebles 1981; van der Leeuw 1981; Hardin 1981; Haddy and Hanson 1981; Powell 1984, 1988; Pope 1989). Their results will be reviewed elsewhere in this report when they are germane to the present research.

Even with all the new information, however, there remained several key questions that could not be answered with the extant archaeological data on the Moundville chiefdom. The most important of these, concerning the economic structure of the chiefdom, required excavation data from the outlying settlements. To acquire these data, I directed small-scale excavations in 1983 at the

White site (1Ha7/8), one of the outlying single-mound sites.

Previous Investigations
at the White Site

Within 25 km of Moundville, there are ten sites that have single mounds known to date to the time of the Moundville chiefdom. There are additional extant mounds, as well as historic references to other, now-destroyed mounds, but the dates of these sites have not been established. Another single-mound site 35 km south of Moundville probably dates to this time as well, though its precise chronological and political relationships to the Moundville chiefdom are unknown. In effect, then, ten single-mound sites are thought to be subsidiary to the paramount center at Moundville. As depicted in figure 3.4, from three to six of these subsidiary sites were occupied at any one time. Cemetery areas at two of the sites were excavated in the 1930s, but aside from extremely small-scale stratigraphic tests and an occasional salvaged burial, surface collections provided the only other artifactual data from these sites available by 1982. Obviously, further excavation was desirable for any investigation of the economic structure of the chiefdom.

I selected the White site (1Ha7/8 in the Alabama state site file) for further excavation. The principal advantage of this site over the other subsidiary centers was that it is the only one that had not suffered deep plowing around the mound; hence it was the site most likely to retain unmixed and stratified deposits. The second advantage was that it is one of the two sites at which cemeteries were excavated in the 1930s, thus allowing me to focus on the residential and midden deposits. The two main disadvantages of the site were its heavy forest cover and the difficulty of getting to and from the site. Both of these disadvantages turned out to be more severe than anticipated and caused considerable delays in both fieldwork and analysis. On the other hand, we located and excavated types of deposits that probably no longer exist at any of the other subsidiary sites.

The White site is located on a relict levee at the south end of an oxbow lake, 0.5 km from the present channel of the Black Warrior River (see figure 3.5). The oxbow lake is labeled as Martin Creek on the USGS Moundville West 7.5′ topographic map, but it was known as Big Heddleston Lake in the 1930s and is currently referred to locally as Whites Swamp. While no geomorphic data are available, the oxbow probably was not the active river channel at the time of mound construction and use. The lowest levee deposits contain fiber-tempered ceramics (1200–500 B.C. [Jenkins 1981, 164]). Had the oxbow been the active river channel during the past 3,000 years, it is unlikely that these deposits would have survived riverbank erosion and channel migration. The levee deposit is fine sandy loam up to 50 cm thick, atop sandy clay that is strongly mottled with iron-manganese oxide staining. The levee may still be accumulating, since at least the lower portions of the site are flooded on a more or less annual basis. Such floods usually occur in January through April (nearly 80 percent of 198 floods recorded at Tuscaloosa from 1888 to 1960 [Peirce 1962, 44–45]), though it was a late May flood that washed out the access road to the site in 1983 and caused much of our difficulty in getting to the site that summer.

The site's susceptibility to flooding was also noted in the first published report of archaeological research at the site. Clarence B. Moore steamed up the Black Warrior River in the spring of 1905 and dug into the mounds at five of the Moundville chiefdom subsidiary sites, including the White site (Moore's "mound near

Bohannon's Landing, Hale County"—Moore 1905, 127, 243–44). He described evidence that spring flooding had covered the ground around the mound to a depth of 8 ft. (2.4 m). He went on to describe the dimensions of the

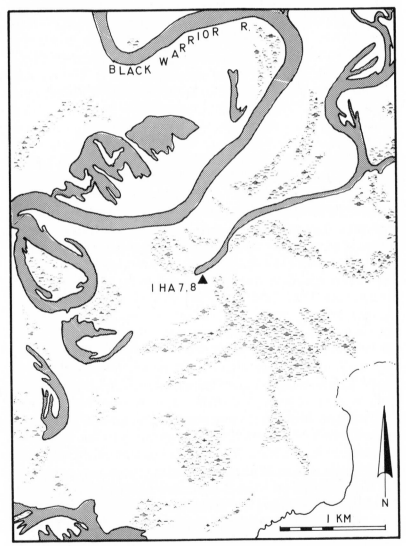

Figure 3.5 Location of the White Site

mound and noted that "considerable digging [on the mound summit] to a depth of from 4 to 5 feet yielded in one place fragments of a human skull" (Moore 1905, 127). Moore's excavations into other mounds at the Moundville subsidiary sites were similarly unproductive. At the time of Moore's visit, the White site was in "a clearing . . . in high swamp, where is a deserted house, and, nearby, the mound with a small building upon it" (Moore 1905, 127). The small building was to play a prominent role in the next recorded excavation at the site.

The next excavation came in the winter of 1930–31, when the site was visited by a field party of the Alabama Museum of Natural History (AMNH). The party consisted of Walter B. Jones, director of the AMNH, and his assistant, David L. DeJarnette. Though Dr. Jones's devotion to the prehistory of the Moundville area cannot be doubted, it seems equally clear that he enjoyed duck hunting, for Jones rented the cabin on the mound and duck hunting rights from the landowner, J. H. White (James F. White, personal communication). DeJarnette's enthusiasm for duck hunting, it seems, was outshone by his dedication to prehistory, for while Jones went hunting, DeJarnette directed excavation in an area northeast of the mound (Tandy Bozeman, personal communication; James F. White, personal communication; unpublished notes on file, Mound State Monument). According to James F. White, son of the landowner and a child at the time, the excavation was prompted by the appearance of a burial eroding out of the large gully on the east side of the mound. The excavation eventually uncovered twenty-nine burials.

The AMNH excavation took place before DeJarnette went to the University of Chicago field school, where he learned more sophisticated recording techniques. Record keeping at the White site was limited to noting whether individual artifacts were associated with a burial, and if so, which one. No map of the excavations nor drawings of the burials were made, and the only surviving information about the location of the excavations is the remark that "one small area about 25 ft. in diameter had skeletons with associated artifacts. Found other skeletons but nothing associated with them" (unpublished notes on file, Mound State Monument). The artifact inventory provides additional information about the burials, such as depth, orientation, and often an assessment of whether the individual was a child or adult. The mortuary remains are described in more detail later in this chapter, so it suffices here to observe that nearly all the artifacts in the inventory are still in the AMNH collections. The skeletal remains, however, appear to have been discarded or lost in the AMNH collections.

It is not clear from the available documents whether the AMNH field party conducted excavations on the mound summit. If so, nothing was found. The mound today preserves evidence of several different excavations, probably Moore's 1905 work and several more recent excavations. No information about the more recent excavations was forthcoming from local residents.

The third recorded visit to the site by archaeologists came in the winter of 1972–73. Jerry Nielsen, John O'Hear, and Charles Moorehead of the University of Alabama relocated the site and collected a small sample of artifacts from the logging road that crosses the site, as well as digging an unspecified number of shovel tests to determine the depth of the artifact-bearing deposits (Nielsen et al. 1973, 78–82). By describing the occupation around the mound as "a large village," they apparently recognized that the 40-x-80-ft. (12.2-x-24.4-m) dimensions listed by the 1930–31 AMNH party were underestimates, but Nielsen and his colleagues did not provide a size estimate of their own.

Except for casual visits by University of Alabama archaeologists, the next expedition to the White site was in

August 1979, when the site survey and testing crew of Christopher Peebles's University of Michigan Museum of Anthropology (UMMA) Moundville project mapped and tested the mound and attempted to define the site boundaries. The crew was under my direction. We excavated three test units, two on the mound summit and one on the eastern flank of the mound. These excavations showed the mound to have been constructed in two episodes, with a series of superimposed, prepared sand floors atop the initial mound summit. This initial mound summit was 1.5 to 1.6 m above the surrounding ground surface. Though the plan and topography of the initial mound are not known, the second construction episode resulted in a rectangular mound 44 x 36 m at the base, with the long axis very nearly east-west. The mound had a split-level summit, with the 16-x-20-m eastern summit 2.7 m above the surrounding ground surface, and the 8-x-20-m western summit 0.6 m higher. No evidence of structural remains on the mound summits were noted in the extremely limited 1979 test excavations. Had there been mound-top structures, most evidence of them is likely to have been obliterated by 400 years of forest growth and historic disturbance. There is also no visible surface indication of the former presence of the duck-hunting cabin, which was on the upper summit. The mound topography and the location of the test units are shown in figure 3.6.

The 1979 UMMA field party also attempted to determine the location of the site boundaries. Since the site was heavily forested (and, more to the point, the end of the field season was only a few days away), the technique employed for this purpose was "quick and dirty." The south margin of the site was determined by judgmentally placed shovel tests, and this margin was followed around the site by further shovel testing. The locations of these shovel tests were not recorded, and the site boundary determined from them was mapped by pac-

ing. Though no artifact collections were kept to document the point, the maximum extent of the site seemed
to reflect the size and location of Late Woodland occupa-
tion(s), while the Mississippian occupation was of
smaller though unknown size. The site size was estimated as 1.3 ha.

Artifacts from the mound stratigraphic tests, as well
as surface collections from around the mound, were
analyzed by Bozeman (1982, 246–61). Using Steponaitis's (1980) chronology of Moundville ceramics,
Bozeman concluded that the White site had been oc-

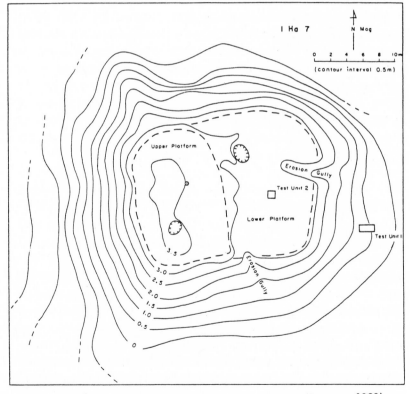

(Bozeman 1982)

Figure 3.6 The White Mound (1Ha7)

cupied, and both initial and final mound construction activities had taken place, during the Moundville III phase. The ceramics—eight whole vessels and 200 sherds—from the 1930–31 AMNH excavations supported this assessment and indicated the presence of minor Moundville I and Protohistoric (Moundville IV) components.

The information about the White site available to me for planning the 1983 excavations can be summarized as follows. The site consisted of a Moundville III occupation smaller than 1.3 ha, overlying more extensive Late Woodland occupation(s). The single platform mound, constructed in two episodes, also dated to the Moundville III phase, as did most or all of the twenty-nine burials excavated in 1930–31. The site was one of six similar Moundville III single-mound sites subsidiary to the multimound paramount center at Moundville.

1983 Excavations at the White Site

Excavation Procedures and Description

Excavation at the White site was conducted from mid-June to late August 1983. It will come as no surprise to fellow archaeologists that the fieldwork actually performed differs from that which was proposed. The research proposal called for a 1-percent sample of the Moundville III phase occupation, using randomly located 2-x-2-m test excavations. This was to be followed by excavation of selected structures and features, assuming such were encountered. In actuality, far less area was excavated than had been proposed. Since the extent of the Moundville III component was far smaller than the site size estimated in 1979, the result was that the excavated area amounted to a 1-percent sample of the Moundville III occupation. A preliminary report (Welch

1983) of the excavation was presented at the South-eastern Archaeological Conference annual meeting in the fall of 1983.

The location of the 1983 excavations are shown in figure 3.7, superimposed on a 0.5-m contour topographic map produced as part of the fieldwork. This map also shows the extent of modern disturbance associated with two access roads that cross the site. The road that runs from the south-southeast to the levee edge was the access road in the early part of this century—possibly the road by which C. B. Moore approached the site. It was replaced as early as the mid-1930s by the road that runs parallel to the levee (viz. Edwards et al. 1939). This road

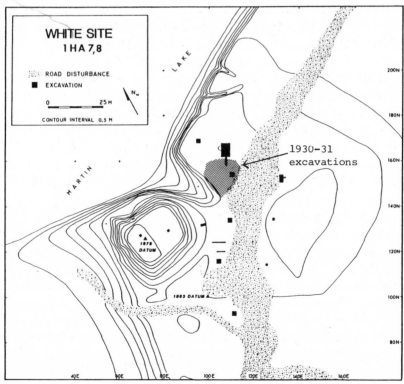

Figure 3.7 The 1983 UMMA Excavations at the White Site

may have been constructed in the 1920s to facilitate logging on the east side of the road. Though the forest east of the road was clear-cut at that time, the timber west of the road was left standing to prevent erosion of the slough edge (James F. White, personal communication). Figure 3.7 also shows the location of the 1979 UMMA mound test excavations and the approximate area of the 1930–31 AMNH burial excavations.

The first step of the fieldwork was the establishment of a site grid. A baseline roughly parallel to the levee edge was set out using transit and tapes. This grid-north baseline was 26°45' east of magnetic north. The locations of all excavation units were designated by the metric grid coordinates of the units' southwest corners. To simplify matters, the grid was labeled so that the entire site was northeast of the grid ON/OE point. In the rest of this chapter, terms such as *north* or *east* refer to grid directions, not magnetic directions.

The research design called for waterscreening of all excavated deposit, using both coarse (¼-in.) and fine (¹⁄₁₆-in.) mesh screens. Flotation samples were also to be taken from all excavation contexts. Excavation provenience was to be recorded at least to 2-x-2-m units, and excavation was to proceed by natural stratigraphy or arbitrary levels not to exceed 10 cm thick. One aspect of this design proved impractical in the field. The fine-mesh waterscreen retained such large quantities of modern rootlets, mast, and leaf litter that it quickly became apparent that some revision of the sampling strategy was necessary. Thenceforth, only one-quarter (usually the southwest quad) of each level in the 2-x-2-m units was fine-screened. The same or larger fraction was used for smaller units. None of the fine-screen samples have been analyzed for this study, though of course all the material has been retained as part of the excavation collection.

One further point about laboratory processing should

be made before proceeding. All of the artifact analysis in this study is based on material retained in ¼-in. screens. This includes the samples from the 1979 UMMA excavations. All the ceramics from the 1983 UMMA excavations were further screened through ½-in. mesh, and the resulting "sherdlets" were not further analyzed. Researchers in this region commonly use this procedure because very small sherds often cannot be classified reliably (e.g., Jenkins 1981; Mann 1983; Steponaitis 1983a).

Test excavation of the White site in 1983 began with excavation of one randomly selected 2-x-2-m square in each 10-m block west of the logging road. By the time the first three units (92N/110E, 115N/103E, 133N/108E) were finished, it was clear that excavation was proceeding more slowly than anticipated, but also that the area south of the mound had no evidence of Moundville III occupation. Attention was focused on the area west of the logging road and north of the mound. Two randomly selected 2-x-2-m units were opened (153N/109E, 168N/94E). In an effort to locate structural remains—house floors or wall trenches—a 10-x-0.5-m trench (158–166N/107E) was excavated across the highest part of this area. This trench revealed a Moundville III midden with good faunal preservation, overlying a partially intact structure floor. A 4-x-6-m block was opened to expose this floor.

Meanwhile, three 1-x-1-m units were excavated east of the road (114N/125E, 134N/128E, 153N/131E). The northernmost unit revealed a short section of a wall trench. In an effort to expose the presumed structure further, excavation at this location was expanded to a 2-x-4.5-m block. No further evidence of the presumed structure was seen. Unfortunately, this excavation proved to be very time-consuming. In retrospect, the effort spent to find a structure at this location would much better have been spent completing the series of 1-x-1-m test excavations east of the logging road. Because of the poor visibility in the undergrowth east of the road, it was only late in the season that the topographic mapping revealed this area to be higher than the area west of the road. It may thus have deeper archaeological deposits and a more complete sequence of occupation than the area west of the road. I consider the lack of adequate test excavation east of the road to be the principal deficiency of the 1983 fieldwork.

Two small (50-x-50-cm) stratigraphic tests were opened to check for possible stratified midden deposits on the slope leading to the slough. In most places, this slope is too steep for debris to accumulate. Accumulation would be possible, however, in the large gully on the north edge of the mound and on the gently sloping ground west of the mound. In both cases, the tests contained sparse artifacts near the surface but were otherwise sterile.

Two additional test trenches, each 50 cm wide, were excavated near the eastern corner of the mound (120N/103–105E and 124N/101–105E). These trenches were an attempt to trace the path of a wide (>1 m) feature that extended northeast-southwest across unit 115N/103E. This feature appeared to be a filled-in ditch extending 40 cm into the sterile clay subsoil. Though the feature extended across the 120N test trench, the situation in the 124N test trench is far from clear. The western end of the 124N test trench intersected a probable sunken house floor bounded by a wall trench. Though this structure probably predates the mound construction, its age is otherwise unknown. The large ditch was not visible. Whether it turned or stopped between the 120N and 124N test trenches is not known. Neither is it clear what the function of the trench was. Conceivably, it is a foundation trench for a palisade around the mound, but it is unusually wide compared to the palisade wall trenches at Moundville (A. Allan 1982; personal communication). A section of the trench was excavated, and of the fifty sherds recovered from the fill, five (10 percent) were shell tempered. This suggests that the feature is of Mississippian date, but more specific information about its age or function is not available.

No excavation of the mound was attempted in the 1983 season. It was felt that the current mound summit would yield no structural data and that artifacts near the surface could not reliably be attributed to fill versus floor contexts. Removal of 1.1 to 1.7 m of overburden to reveal the earlier mound summit was simply not feasible for a small crew with limited time. Excavation of the mound would also require removal of the trees on it, some of which are nearly 1 m in diameter.

History of Occupation at the White Site

Despite the incompleteness of the systematic testing program east of the logging road, the 1983 fieldwork provides considerable information about the history of occupation at the site. In addition to minor occupations of nearly all periods from around 1000 B.C. (a few fiber-tempered sherds were recovered) through A.D. 800, there was a large Late Woodland occupation(s) of the West Jefferson phase (A.D. 850 or 900 to 1050). The location was then unoccupied, or *mostly* unoccupied, for roughly 400 years. Of the more than 20,000 shell-tempered sherds recovered from the site, roughly 20 (0.1 percent) display modes that occur no later than late Moundville II. Occasional farmsteads or perhaps small extractive camps would account for these rare Moundville I and II diagnostics. The site became a focus for occupation again during the Moundville III phase.

It is not clear exactly when in the Moundville III period this occupation began. The uncertainty stems from a variety of sampling and preservation problems. First, if the initial occupation in the Moundville III phase had

been located on the high ground east of the present logging road, the 1983 sampling program would have
missed it. Second, the most characteristic ceramic diagnostics for the periods preceding late Moundville III are
fine-line incised (so-called engraved) motifs executed on
burnished, fine shell-tempered vessels. Except in the
late Moundville III midden, with its relatively good shell
preservation, fine shell-tempered sherds at the White
site tend to have weathered surfaces that would not reveal the (former) presence of such decoration. This
means that the apparent rarity of sherds diagnostically
prior to late Moundville III might be due to their differential destruction.

Table 3.1 Ceramics from the Lower Mound Fill, 1Ha7[1]

Type and variety	Rim sherds no.	%	Body sherds no.	%
Sand tempered				
Baldwin Plain *var. Blubber*	0	0	2	0.3
Unclassified	0	0	1	0.1
Grog tempered				
Baytown Plain *var. Roper*	10	47.6	409	62.0
Mulberry Creek Cordmarked				
var. Aliceville	1	4.8	26	3.9
Wheeler Check Stamped				
var. Sipsey	0	0	1	0.1
Shell tempered				
Mississippi Plain				
var. Warrior	10	47.6	214	32.4
Bell Plain *var. Hale*	0	0	4	0.6
Carthage Incised				
var. Carthage	0	0	1	0.1
Moundville Engraved				
var. unspecified	0	0	2	0.3

[1] From Bozeman (1982, 258-59; and personal communication)

The third source of uncertainty in dating the reoc-
cupation of the site is the possibility that the remains of
this occupation may have been removed. Though there is
no evidence of such removal by natural agencies, the
first stage of the mound was constructed of artifact-
bearing, dark, humic silt. This sediment appears to have
been part of the sheet midden covering the site. I suspect
that the fill for the first mound stage came from the area
south and east of the mound, on the basis of the low ele-
vation and relatively low percentage of shell-tempered
ceramics (0 to 55 percent in the top 10 cm) in this area.
The ceramics in the first mound fill are consistent with
this interpretation. Test Unit 2 of the 1979 excavations
penetrated 1 m into the first mound stage, recovering
681 sherds, of which 34 percent are shell tempered (see
table 3.1). Only three of the shell-tempered sherds were
decorated wares useful for dating within the Moundville

Table 3.2 White Site Burials with Associated Vessels[1]

Burial no.	Vessel no.	Vessel description
2	Wh2	Bell Plain var. *Hale* restricted bowl with 4 equidistant nodes at inflection point, 14 cm diameter x 7 cm high
16	Wh53	Mississippi Plain var. *Warrior* subglobular jar with 20 handles, red paint on interior of rim, 14 cm diameter x 11 cm high
	Wh54	Alabama River Incised water bottle, unburnished, with 3-line running scroll sloppily incised in wet paste, 11 cm diameter x 8 cm high
28	Wh58	Bell Plain var. *Hale* hemispherical bowl with beaded rim, 13 cm diameter x 8 cm high

[1] From unpublished notes on file, Mound State Monument

era. Two of these sherds have the fine-line incising that is notably rare in the off-mound test units and that is most common prior to late Moundville III.

The clearest indication of occupation at the site prior to late Moundville III comes from the 1930–31 AMNH burial excavations. Of the twenty-nine burials excavated, three included ceramic vessels (see table 3.2). Burial 2 was accompanied by a Bell Plain var. *Hale* restricted bowl with widely spaced nodes. In Steponaitis's seriation of grave lots at Moundville, widely spaced nodes on bowls is a mode restricted to late Moundville II and early Moundville III. There are two reasons to be cautious in interpreting this information. In the first place, the date of a burial does not necessarily indicate the date of the site occupation and construction activities. Secondly, a seriation is an approximation to a chronological ordering, and it would be a mistake to place too great reliance on the prospective fit of one item from the White site to a seriation of items from Moundville. Overall, however, the ceramics from the first mound stage and from Burial 2 indicate that the White site may have been reoccupied during the early Moundville III phase.

Most of the occupation at the site, however, dates to the later part of the Moundville III phase. The ceramic diagnostics from the site include beaded rims on bowls, flaring-rim bowls (both shallow and deep), standard jars with eight or more handles, red and white painted pottery, incised hand and eye designs, and Carthage Incised var. *Carthage* (see figure 3.8). This list nearly duplicates the upper end of Steponaitis's seriation of pottery from Moundville (Steponaitis 1983a, figure 26). Burnished subglobular bottles, and the type Moundville Engraved, are almost absent from the site. The late Moundville III ceramic assemblage was present in every excavation unit north of the 130N grid line, although, with one exception described below, every excavation *[handwritten margin note: I think this is expected, if one takes a functional temporal view (not an episodic replacement view) ceramic change.]*

level also contained at least 10-percent admixture of Late Woodland ceramics. Arguments are presented above that some part of the area south of the 130N grid line may also have been occupied during part of the Moundville III phase.

Bell Plain <u>var.</u>
<u>Hale</u> or <u>Big</u> <u>Sandy</u>
beaded rim bowl

Carthage Incised
<u>var.</u> <u>Moon</u> <u>Lake</u>
short-neck bowl

Mississippi Plain
<u>var.</u> <u>Warrior</u>
standard jar
8+ handles

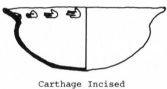

Carthage Incised
<u>var.</u> <u>Fosters</u>
flaring rim bowl

← red
← white

Unclassified
red and white painted
short-neck bowl

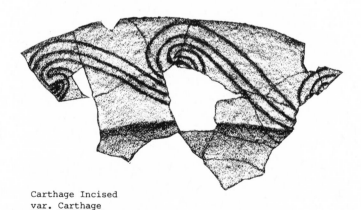

Carthage Incised
<u>var.</u> <u>Carthage</u>
rim of flaring rim bowl

Figure 3.8 Ceramic Modes from the White Site

Taking this possibility into account, a maximum size
for the late Moundville III component can be calculated
(see figure 3.9). Though the extent of the component
east of the logging road is not definitely known, occupation on land below the 0.0-m contour of figure 3.9 is
highly unlikely, as soil below this contour is very poorly
drained. Using the 0.0-m contour as the effective site
boundary, the site is 0.74 ha. This estimate includes the
area of the mound (0.17 ha). Excluding the mound, the
occupation area amounts to 0.57 ha.

The sampling fraction attained by the 1983 excavations can be calculated using this site size estimate.

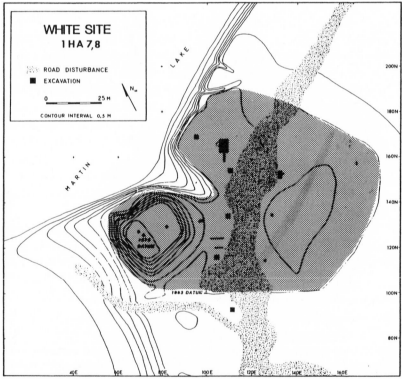

Figure 3.9 Maximum Extent of Late Moundville III Occupation at
White

Within the estimated site boundary 55.5 m² were excavated. This is just under 1 percent of the off-mound occupation area. It is also worth noting that the area disturbed by the logging road is 0.13 ha, or 23 percent of the site.

The spatial organization of the late Moundville III community at the White site cannot be determined with the present data. That is, the number, nature, and distribution of structures are not known. Clearly, the structure(s) atop the mound was symbolically and presumably functionally distinct from those elsewhere at the site. It is also clear from the 1930–31 AMNH excavations that an area near the northeast flank of the mound was a cemetery area. The area southeast of the mound, from which the first mound fill may have come, has very sparse late Moundville III ceramics and therefore may have been a plaza area. Since this argument relies more on an absence of evidence than on the presence of any positive criteria, little faith should be attached to it. Furthermore, there is no visible ramp leading from this possible plaza to the mound summit. In fact, the only ramplike feature of the mound descends from the northwest corner of the mound toward the slough edge (see figure 3.5). This is diagonally opposite the cemetery area and the zone of sheet midden that probably indicates the residential area.

Within the residential zone, one small area is quantitatively, if not qualitatively, distinct. This is the low rise around 166N/105E. This rise is an accumulation of late Moundville III midden roughly 20 cm thick. A 4-x-6-m block of this deposit was excavated. The largely unmixed late Moundville III midden blankets a mixed Moundville/Late Woodland midden such as found elsewhere on the site. The density of artifacts in the late Moundville III midden (up to 7,800 sherds per cubic meter) is twice that found elsewhere at the site. It is the only area of the site with identifiable faunal remains.

The late Moundville III midden also contains items rare or absent elsewhere at the site, e.g., fragments of greenstone celts, fragments of notched sandstone discs (such as the "paint palettes" found at Moundville; see Webb and DeJarnette 1942, 287–91), and pieces of galena. Immediately underlying the midden in the excavation block is a fragmentary structure floor. Badly disturbed by 400 years of tree roots and rodent burrows, the floor is present only in patches. Where present, these patches have piles of sherds lying flat atop the floor. These are deposits of broken pottery brought to this location for discard, not collapsed, in situ vessels. On the basis of the density of cultural debris and the character of the artifacts lying on the floor, the late Moundville III midden is interpreted as an intentional refuse deposit—a trash dump—rather than the chance accumulation of debris seen elsewhere at the site.

The White site was abandoned at the end of the Moundville III phase or very early in the Protohistoric era. Three sherds of Alabama River Appliqué, one sherd of Alabama River Incised (Sheldon 1974, 203–6 [or Mississippi Plain var. *Hull Lake* with applied handles, and Barton Incised var. *Big Prairie* in the scheme of Curren 1982]), and one whole vessel of Alabama River Incised (or Barton Incised var. *Big Prairie*) found with Burial 16 are the only Protohistoric diagnostics recovered from the AMNH and UMMA excavations. This indicates that the White site was abandoned at very nearly the same time that Moundville itself ceased to be occupied. Steponaitis (1983a, 126) estimated this date at roughly A.D. 1550. This estimate is corroborated by material from the 1983 UMMA excavations.

Four absolute dates were obtained from the area of the refuse deposit (see tables 3.3 and 3.4). A radiocarbon date from a smudge pit stratigraphically below the structure floor yielded an uncalibrated, $^{13}C/^{12}C$-corrected estimate of a.d. 1320 ± 50. This date is considered

Table 3.3 Radiocarbon Dates from the White Site

Lab no.	Sample description	Years b.p. 5568 half life	$^{13}C/^{12}C$ (0/00)	$^{13}C/^{12}C$ adjusted years b.p.	Adjusted years b.p. 5730 half life	Calibrated[1] 95% confidence interval A.D.
Beta 9952	Pine and oak charcoal, possibly with some maize; Fea. 56 (162N/105E); Moundville II/III	670 ± 50	-27.38	630 ± 50	650 ± 50	1260-1405 (midpoint = A.D. 1335)
Beta 9951	Pine and hardwood charcoal; 164N/105E L.2; late Moundville III	400 ± 50	-	-	410 ± 50	1405-1620 (midpoint = A.D. 1515)

[1] Klein et al. (1982) calibration

Table 3.4 Thermoluminescence Dates from the White Site

Lab no.	Sample description	Years B.P.	Date A.D.
Alpha 1231	Carthage Incised var. *Carthage* rim sherd; 164N/105E L.2; late Moundville III	430 ± 50	1520 ± 50
Alpha 1232	Bell Plain var. *Hale* short-neck bowl rim sherd; 164N/105E L.2; late Moundville III	420 ± 40	1530 ± 40

acceptable for the ceramic associations. A radiocarbon determination was made on wood charcoal loose in the refuse deposit. The sample was drawn from 10 to 20 cm below ground surface in the excavation unit in which the underlying structure floor was most intact. The uncorrected date is a.d. 1550 ± 50. Using the calibration tables of Klein et al. (1982), the midpoint of the 95-percent confidence interval for the true date is around A.D. 1515. Two sherds from the same excavation context were dated by thermoluminescence, with the background radiation dose rate calibrated from an associated sediment sample. A late Moundville III diagnostic short-neck bowl rim was dated at A.D. 1530 ± 40. The other sherd was a piece of the Carthage Incised var. *Carthage* rim illustrated in figure 3.8 (the illustrated rim is composed of fifteen sherds, all recovered from this excavation level). The estimated date is A.D. 1520 ± 50.

These three dates on late Moundville III material are the first acceptable absolute dates acquired for this phase (an A.D. 1840 ± 50 date from Moundville is obviously inaccurate—Steponaitis 1983a, 126; M. Scarry, personal communication, 1986). They accord well with the mid-sixteenth- and seventeenth-century dates for the ensuing Protohistoric period (e.g., Curren 1982, 109; 1984, 89–193). Since the dated material comes from the later part of the Moundville III phase, and from near the end of the White site occupation, these dates indicate that occupation at both the White site and Moundville ceased very close to A.D. 1540, the year De Soto's army passed across western Alabama.

Data Used in the Analysis

For data from the Moundville chiefdom to be useful in evaluating the alternative models of chiefdom economic structure, the data available in 1982 needed to be supplemented with excavated material from one of the subsidiary centers. In this chapter, I have described the White site excavations, but I have not yet specifically addressed the issue of whether the excavations produced data with the qualities necessary for my purposes. The excavations *did* produce data with the necessary qualities, but not all of the excavations were successful in this sense. The primary quality desired of the data is that they not be chronologically mixed. Mixed Late Woodland and Moundville deposits, after all, would not be significantly more useful than the published, similarly mixed, surface collection data from other sites. Mixed ceramics, of course, can be sorted out by component, but the lithic, faunal, and botanical data cannot. Only one area of the White site yielded unmixed Moundville-era deposits—the late Moundville III refuse deposit around 164N/107E. With few exceptions, the White site data used in this analysis have come from the 4-x-6-m excavation of this refuse deposit. Since so much reliance is placed on these data, it is necessary to clarify as much as possible what this deposit represents in terms of the White site community and the chiefdom as a whole.

It is not possible to specify which households within the community deposited refuse in this location. In part, this stems from the near absence of identifiable structures in the excavations. Even if preserved floors and wall trench patterns had been encountered, it is still not likely that the origin of the refuse could be determined.

Though we cannot specify where the refuse came from physically, the material itself contains some indications of where it came from in sociological terms. That is, we can determine what kind of households contributed to the refuse deposit. From the distribution of items in graves at Moundville, and the location of the graves within that site, we know that certain items and raw materials were restricted to the (ascriptive) upper stratum of Moundville society. Among these were stone discs ("paint palettes") and galena cubes (Peebles 1974; Peebles and Kus 1977, 439). Two pieces of galena and at least one fragment of a notched sandstone disc were included in the late Moundville III refuse deposit at the White site. Neither kind of artifact was encountered elsewhere at the site. This suggests that the household(s) of the local elite contributed to the refuse deposit.

Households of lower status probably also deposited refuse at this location. If only the elite household(s) were piling trash in this area, it is likely that the ratio of serving and storage vessels to cooking vessels would be higher than the ratio elsewhere at the site. This implication follows from the well-known obligation of hospitality on the part of chiefs or people of high rank (Sahlins 1972, 268, 270). This obligation would lead to a "different balance of functions performed in households of varying statuses" (Drennan 1975, 135). Whalen (1976, 117) and Drennan (1975, 135), for example, showed that the serving:cooking ratios were higher in debris from high-status households than from low-status households in Formative villages in Oaxaca. The ratio of serving to cooking wares in the White site refuse deposit is slightly lower than the ratio elsewhere at the site, as shown in table 3.5 (excavation units with combined sample sizes below fifty are discounted here, due to the potentially high sampling error). On this basis, it seems that the elite household(s) was not the only nor even necessarily the major producer(s) of the refuse. Though spatially only a small part of the site, the refuse deposit is a sample of the refuse from a broad (though perhaps not complete) portion of the community.

In order for the refuse data to be relevant to questions about the economic structure of a complex chiefdom, the data must be shown to date to a time when the Moundville system was still functioning as a complex chiefdom. This is an obvious point, but the data are from a time so close to the disintegration of the Moundville chiefdom that the point is far from trivial. There are two avenues along which this issue may be approached: comparison of late Moundville III burials at Moundville and at White, and comparison of the extent of occupation at the two sites. The latter avenue will be traveled first.

The very incomplete available information on the extent of late Moundville III occupation at Moundville indicates that this occupation was both qualitatively and quantitatively different from that at White. Since the vast corpus of artifacts excavated at Moundville has not been reanalyzed in light of Steponaitis's ceramic chronology, this conclusion is tentative. Nevertheless, we know that there are late Moundville III burials and midden deposits at several locations around the plaza (Steponaitis 1983a, 90; Welch 1989; see figure 3.10). This suggests that in late Moundville III times, Moundville

Table 3.5 Ratios of Serving to Cooking Wares by Excavation Unit

Excavation unit	No. of Mississippi Plain sherds (cooking ware)	No. of burnished or painted sherds (serving ware)	Serving to cooking ratio
Refuse deposit[1]	13619	3304	.24
168N/94E[2]	78	17	.22
153N/109E[3]	404	109	.27
East block	1330	373	.28
134N/128E	70	22	.31
133N/108E	27	4	.15
Other units[4]	16	0	0

[1] Includes only material from Level 1 (0-10 cm below surface); additional material below this level cannot be reliably sorted due to erosion and encrustation of surfaces.
[2] Only Levels 1-4 included; other levels are fill in modern trench.
[3] Comprises contiguous units in the northernmost excavations east of the roadway
[4] Comprises units south of 135N west of the roadway

had a large population living around the very large central plaza.

The sample of excavated burials also suggests that the late Moundville III population residing at Moundville was larger than that residing at White. Thirty burials at Moundville, comprising fifty individuals, contain vessels diagnostic of the late Moundville III phase (Steponaitis 1983a, table 35; Peebles 1979). Table 3.6 presents summary information about these burials. In contrast, only two burials at White included late Moundville III diagnostic vessels (see table 3.7). Since a larger fraction of Moundville has been excavated than of White—5 percent (Peebles 1978a, 375) versus roughly 2 percent (55 m^2 in 1983 plus an estimated 50 m^2 in 1930–31)—the comparison should be adjusted accordingly. (The site information form filled out by either Jones or DeJarnette for the White site in the 1930s has a comment after the heading "Possibility of further excavation": "We thought we had it all" [unpublished document on file, Mound State Monument].) If we further assume that all twenty-nine individuals at White were buried in the late Moundville III phase, this figure is still small, relative to the number of burials at Moundville that might date to the same time: of those burials that included vessels, roughly 370 may date as late as late Moundville III, and there are 1,256 burials with no vessels and hence no assigned date (Steponaitis 1983a, table 35; Peebles 1979). If these 1,600 + loosely dated burials have the same date distribution as the 95 burials with definite dates, roughly 20 percent (or 320) should be late Moundville III burials. There are other ways of manipulating these numbers, but even with the most conservative assumptions, the number of known plus likely late Moundville III burials at Moundville equals several times the number from White.

Though Moundville's population was much larger than White's at this time, political relations between

Table 3.6 Summary Data on Late Moundville III Burials at Moundville[1]

Burial no.	Orientation (head toward)	Age & sex[2]	Single or multiple	Associated artifacts
1956/Rho	- - -	Adult	Multiple (1956-7/Rho)	Water bottle (141Rho) Sherds (143Rho) Hammerstone (144Rho)
1957/Rho	- - -	Adult	"	Broken pot (142Rho) Sherds (143Rho) Hammerstone (145Rho)
2086/Rho	- - -	Adult	Single	Water bottle (304Rho) Water bottle (305Rho) Bowl (306Rho) Human effigy bowl (307Rho) Water bottle (308Rho) Water bottle (309Rho) Water bottle (310Rho)
(11)/D/M5	- - -	- - -	Multiple (11 skulls plus other bones)	Narrow-neck bottle (D1/M5) Canine (?) effigy bowl Small undecorated wide-mouth bottle Undecorated vessel Undecorated vessel

53/NE	---	---	Single	Plain pot with 12 handles (14NE)
1611/NE	South	Young child	Multiple (1611-3/NE)	Bowl (185NE)
1612/NE	South	Adult male (>40, male)	"	Water bottle fragment (186NE)
1613/NE	South	Adult male (30-35, female)	"	---
1180/EE	---	---	Multiple (1180-4/EE, 1193/EE)	(Plow disturbed)
1181/EE	East	Adult (35-40, female)	"	Incised bowl (3EE) 2 long bone awls (57EE)
1182/EE	East	Adult	"	Incised water bottle (1EE) Notched-rim bowl (2EE)
1183/EE	East	Adult	"	Water bottle (4EE) 2 beads (26EE)
1184/EE	---	Child (5-10)	"	Water bottle (6EE)
1193/EE	East	Adult	"	--- [Also one incised water bottle not attributable to any one individual]

(Table 3.6, *continued*)

Burial no.	Orientation (head toward)	Age & sex [2]	Single or multiple	Associated artifacts
1213/EE	East	Adult (40-45, male)	Multiple (1213-5/EE)	Beaded-rim bowl (61EE) Bone implement (62EE) Water bottle (63EE) Fragment of pot (64EE) 2 shell beads (65EE) (accidental inclusion?--fragment of greenstone ax [66EE])
1214/EE	North	Adult (40-45, female)	"	- - -
1215/EE	- - -	Infant or small child (0-6 months)	"	- - -
1233/EE	West	Adult (40-45, female)	Multiple (1233-7/EE, 1245-7/EE)	This multiple burial was a mass of bones (1234-7/EE) at the feet of 1233/EE. In the same pit, but below and apparently disturbed by these, were 1245-7/EE. Artifacts included in the multiple burial are: water bottle (85EE)
1234/EE	- - -	- - -	"	
1235/EE	- - -	- - -	"	

1236/EE	---	---	"	water bottle (86EE) red-filmed bowl (87EE)
1237/EE	---	---	"	bowl (88EE)
1245/EE	---	---	"	crushed pot (89EE)
1246/EE	---	Adult (45-50, male)	"	pottery fragments from fill (90-93EE)
1247/EE	---	---	"	
1261/EE	North	Child	Single	Pot (124EE) Small bowl, red-filmed int. (125EE) Small incised bowl (126EE) 15 shell beads (127EE)
1291/EE	Northeast	Adult	Multiple (1291-2/EE)	Large sherd (202EE) Animal head effigy bowl (203EE)
1292/EE	---	---	"	Water bottle (204EE)
843/EI	East	Adult	Single	Incised short-neck bowl (39EI) Jar with >10 handles (40EI) Incised bottle (41EI)

(Table 3.6, *continued*)

Burial no.	Orientation (head toward)	Age & sex[2]	Single or multiple	Associated artifacts
1718/SWG	- - -	- - -	Single	Undecorated water bottle (6SWG) Crushed pot (SWG)
1720/SWG	- - -	Child	Single	Bowl (8SWG)
1725/SWG	- - -	Adult female (35-40, female)	Single	Fragments of bowl (9SWG) Fragments of human effigy head bowl (10SWG)
947/SWM	(bundle)	- - -	Single	Carved stone disc (86SWM) Burnished jar with widely spaced nodes (87SWM) Galena (88SWM)
1160/SWM	South	Child (1.5-2.0)	Single	Shell beads (249-250SWM) Stone pendant (251SWM) Short-neck bowl (252SWM) Galena (253SWM) Bone awl (254SWM)

2417/WP	North	Adult (30-35, female)	Multiple (w/2449/WP)	Incised bowl (121WP) Red and white painted bowl (122WP)
2449/WP	---	Child (1-5)	Multiple (w/2417/WP)	Shell beads (123WP) 2 shell earplugs (124WP)
2768/RW (69+05 L2)	Southeast	Adult	Single	Bowl fragments (195RW) Pottery effigy pipe (189RW)

1 Data from Peebles (1979) and V. Steponaitis (personal communication)
2 Parenthesized age and sex information from M. Powell (personal communication)

Table 3.7 Summary Data on Late Moundville III Burials at White[1]

Burial no.	Orientation (head toward)	Age & sex	Associated artifacts and excavators' comments
1	- - -	- - -	- - -
2	West	Small child about 3 yrs old	Carinated bowl with widely spaced nodes (Wh2) placed at right knee
3	- - -	- - -	4 perforated bear teeth (Wh3) at neck
4	- - -	- - -	- - -
5	Southeast	Adult male	Sandstone disc (Wh4), 7 cm diameter, at foot
6	- - -	- - -	- - -
7	East	About 6' tall	4 perforated bear teeth (Wh5) at left wrist Sandstone disc (Wh6), 10 cm diameter, at left hand "Also paint, shells, whatnot"
8-13	- - -	- - -	[These were separate burials, no further information recorded]
14	East	Infant	- - -
15	North	Child	Shell pendant (Wh50), poorly preserved

16	East	Probably 2 yrs old	Shell beads (Wh51) at wrist and neck; Copper ornament (Wh52) on chest, badly decayed; Plain jar with 20 handles (Wh53) at right of skull, inverted on: Alabama River Incised bottle (Wh54)
16a	East	---	---
17	---	Infant	---
18	East	About 6 yrs	Fragments of decayed wood at feet
19	East	Infant	Sherd discoidal (Wh56) at hips
20	---	Adult	---
21	East	---	"Bones taken out," i.e., by the excavators
22	---	Infant	"Bone last stages of decay"
23	South	---	"Bones charred"
24	East	---	"In very bad shape"
25	South	---	"In very bad shape"
26	East	---	---
27	South	---	---
28	---	Infant	Beaded rim bowl (Wh58) at left of skull

1 From unpublished notes on file, Mound State Monument

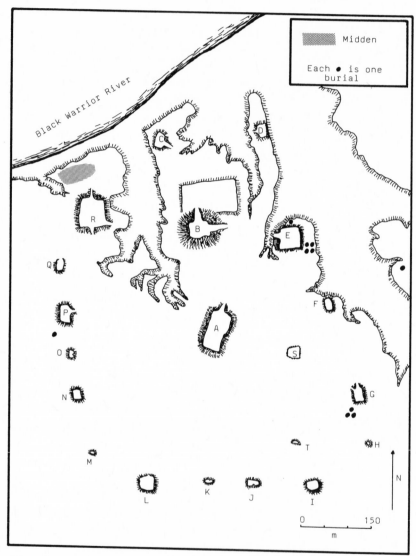

Figure 3.10 Location of Late Moundville III Material at Moundville

their occupants were not necessarily those of a complex chiefdom. Moundville was in its decline, as measured by the number of burials made, amount of mound construction, and average number of imported items per burial (Steponaitis 1983a, 151–61; Peebles 1987a). It is difficult to determine how far this decline had progressed at the time the refuse deposit at White was being formed. The most obvious approach is to examine the chronological distribution of burials in Peebles's (1972, 1974; Peebles and Kus 1977) cluster analysis.

Peebles distinguished ten groups of similar burials at Moundville. In eight of these, the burials of males contrast with those of females, and infants and children contrast with adults. These burials are interpreted as representing "commoner" status, or the subordinate dimension of status variability at Moundville. The other two groups of burials are spatially isolated from the rest of the population and associated with sets of artifacts that are not patterned by age or gender distinctions. These burials are interpreted as the "nobility" of the society. A subset of seven adult males (though sex determinations were not made by trained osteologists) were buried in mounds, with copper axes, pearl beads, and copper-covered wooden beads as grave goods. These are thought to be deceased paramount chiefs. The only one of these seven burials that can be dated had vessels of the late Moundville II period. Three of the burials that definitely date to late Moundville III were members of the nobility, but in each case, this was only by virtue of the presence of a few shell beads in the burial. To summarize, only three "nobles" demonstrably were buried at Moundville in late Moundville III times, and none of them had particularly "rich" burials. In contrast, three burials at White contained artifacts that would place these burials among the nobility at Moundville, and one of these burials included a copper ornament. Only one of these three is definitely dated as late as late Moundville III, however.

To restate this information, in the late Moundville III phase, the occupation at Moundville was several or many times the size of that at White, yet there was a greater proportion of noble burials, and perhaps a burial of higher nobility, at White than at Moundville. Since the majority of noble burials at Moundville have not been dated, there is not necessarily any discrepancy here. Given these facts, my interpretation is that in the later part of the Moundville III phase, the chiefdom was declining in terms of access to nonlocal materials. Nevertheless, the society was still organized as a complex chiefdom, with Moundville as the paramount center.

At this point, it may help the reader to have a brief, jargon-free description of the White site. It was a small cluster of no more than twenty households, grouped around a mound. There were one or more structures on top of the mound, wherein lived the highest ranking member(s) of the local community. An unknown, but presumably large, number of households were scattered around the countryside within a few kilometers of the White site; this dispersed population probably regarded the White site as the focus of most of their daily social interaction. The White community, including the dispersed households, was one of six similar districts occupying the floodplain north and south of Moundville. All of the people in these districts probably regarded Moundville as the "capital" of their society, the locus of the highest level of political leadership, and the site of the principal religious ceremonies. Through time, the ties that made the White community subsidiary to the Moundville leadership may have weakened, though they were not severed until after the period when the late Moundville III refuse was deposited.

The final task of this chapter is to describe the manner

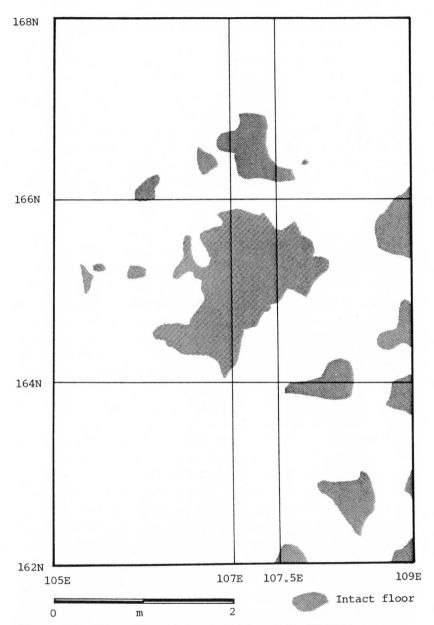

Figure 3.11 Map of Floor below Late Moundville III Midden

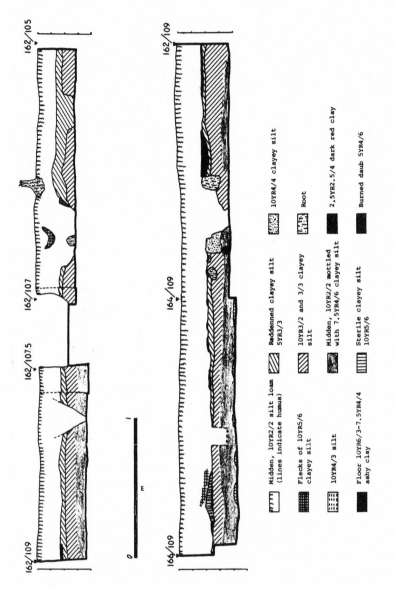

Figure 3.12 Representative Profiles from Excavation of Refuse Deposit

in which the refuse deposit excavation contexts are grouped into the analytic units that will be used throughout this study. The refuse deposit (see figures 3.11 and 3.12) was excavated in three levels. The top two levels were each 10-cm arbitrary levels. The third level comprised the material from 20 cm below surface to the floor level. Artifacts lying flat on the floor were left in situ and provenienced separately from the Level 3 artifacts. The floor itself was excavated and washed through windowscreen or processed by flotation. No artifacts ¼ in. (0.6 cm) or larger were present; the only artifacts present were small flecks of pottery, bone, shell, and charred botanical material. Below the floor level was a mixed Late Woodland/Mississippian midden, which was excavated in a combination of natural stratigraphic and arbitrary levels. Since only scant reference will be made to the subfloor data, and even then to these data as a single set, no further description of the subfloor excavation is necessary here.

For the analysis of the White site refuse data, there are four analytical dimensions by which the data can be grouped. Three of these dimensions have already been mentioned: excavation unit (e.g., 164N/107E); above versus below floor; and excavation layer (e.g., Level 1 or 0 to 10 cm below surface). The fourth dimension is the degree of disturbance of the deposits. Since there was no significant accumulation of cultural debris after the late Moundville III period, the principal concern is the extent to which the late Moundville III data have been contaminated with earlier materials from below the floor. Poorer preservation of the earlier faunal and botanical material may minimize this problem for these two classes of data. The situation for lithics, however, is quite different. Relatively pure Late Woodland contexts at the site typically have three to five times more lithic items than sherds, while the proportion is exactly the reverse in relatively pure late Moundville III contexts. This means, for instance, that in a provenience unit with 5-percent admixture of Late Woodland ceramics, up to 50 percent of the lithics may be of Late Woodland origin. The late Moundville III refuse deposit typically has 3- to 10-percent admixture of pre-Mississippian sherds. Effectively, then, the lithic sample is heavily contaminated.

For nonlithic classes of data, however, a maximum of 10-percent admixture of pre-Mississippian ceramics is the criterion for accepting provenience lots for analysis. This cutoff point is arbitrary but is defensible in light of the pattern of provenience units that do not meet it. The two units that do not meet the criterion are the top 10 cm of 166N/107E and 166N/107.5E. The northern end of these units borders a ditchlike surface feature. Whether the feature is natural or artificial is not known, but the high proportion of pre-Mississippian sherds in the surface deposits beside it suggests that the ditch was dug and the spoil deposited alongside it.

This chapter can be summarized by repeating the main points. The prehistoric Moundville chiefdom is well known archaeologically, but to be suitable for evaluating models of chiefdom economic structure, additional data were needed from a subsidiary center. Excavations at the White site produced many artifacts, but most of the contexts were chronologically mixed. Relatively unmixed late Moundville III refuse was encountered in one area. The refuse seems to have been produced by a combination of elite and nonelite households. The refuse was deposited at a time when the Moundville chiefdom was in decline, but the limited information available suggests that the Black Warrior River valley population was still organized as a complex chiefdom. The refuse data can be examined in terms of horizontal coordinates, depth from surface, position relative to the underlying structure floor, and degree of contamination by earlier materials. The most extensively mixed contexts, i.e., those with more than 10-percent pre-Mississippian sherds, are eliminated from the subsequent analyses. Full artifact tabulations for all excavation contexts can be found in Welch (1986, appendix A).

4 Subsistence

Introduction

The production, distribution, and consumption of food is a vital sector of any economy. Thus, it seems a good place to begin an examination of the economic structure of a chiefdom. The redistribution model and the mobilization model posit very different ways for the subsistence sector to be organized. The redistribution model envisions a chiefdom composed of units that have quite different resources and products, but which, through the action of a central "distributor," each receive a portion of other units' products. The mobilization model envisions a chiefdom composed of similar self-sufficient units. Aside from occasional "famine relief," the principal movement of food across unit boundaries is the movement of food from domestic producers to the elite. In this chapter, I compare these contrasting models with subsistence data from the Moundville chiefdom.

Several kinds of data are examined. First, the location of the units of the chiefdom is considered: are they in similar or contrasting locations with respect to food resources? In the Moundville case, the units of the chiefdom are the single-mound subsidiary sites with their neighborhoods of dispersed farmsteads. Other data I examine are the physical remains of foods and their by-products. Both animal and plant food remains have been recovered from the White subsidiary site and from the paramount center at Moundville. The faunal data are examined first. Due to the small size of the analyzed faunal sample from Moundville, much of the faunal analysis involves comparisons between White and two Mississippian sites that are nearby but were not Moundville subsidiaries. The plant food data from Moundville are of higher quality than the faunal data, and in the section dealing with botanical data, the comparisons are restricted to sites within the Moundville chiefdom. Site location data are examined separately for faunal procurement and procurement of plant foods.

Fauna

Though faunal remains were not found in most portions of the White site, they were present in the late Moundville III refuse deposit. Within this deposit, faunal preservation varied from negligible in the top 5 cm of soil, to very good in undisturbed deposits above the structure floor, which was approximately 25 cm below surface. All faunal remains from the refuse deposit, including those from below the floor, were identified to gross taxonomic category (e.g., small mammal, bird, turtle) by Scott Blanchard, using comparative collections of the Museum of Anthropology and the Museum of Zoology, University of Michigan. Small mammal remains were further identified, to species when possible. The large mammal remains were also subjected to extensive further analysis, detailed below. The poor preservation, small sample size, and chronologically mixed nature of the subfloor samples make it extremely difficult to extract useful information from these earlier materials. Throughout the following discussion, therefore, I include only the faunal material from above the floor and in excavation units with minimally mixed ceramics (as explained in chapter three; see Welch 1986, appendix B, for complete listing of all faunal data).

Within the faunal sample from unmixed contexts above the floor, differential preservation of bone does not appear to be a significant factor. Light, spongy bone generally is destroyed more rapidly than dense, solid bone, so that differential bone preservation typically results in assemblages dominated by dense skeletal elements (Lyman 1985). In the White site refuse deposit bone assemblage, there is only a low correlation between density of skeletal element and abundance of element (Kendall's tau-b = 0.24, p = 0.27, see figure 4.1 and table 4.1; bone density values and analytical procedures from Lyman 1985).

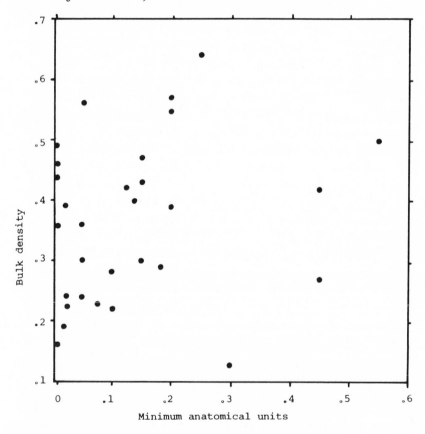

Figure 4.1 Scatterplot of Deer Bone Density and Abundance

Table 4.1 White Site Deer Skeletal Element Abundances and Bone
Density Values

Skeletal element	No. of elements observed	No. in whole animal	MAU[1]	Bulk density[2]
Mandible	4	2	2.00	0.57
Atlas	3	1	3.00	0.13
Axis	0	1	0	0.16
Cervical vert.	1	5	0.20	0.19
Thoracic vert.	3	13	0.23	0.24
Lumbar vert.	11	6	1.83	0.29
Innominate	9	2	4.50	0.27
Sacrum	0	1	0	0.19
Rib	36	26	1.38	0.40
Sternum	1	1	1.00	0.22
Scapula	0	2	0	0.36
P. humerus	1	2	0.50	0.24
D. humerus	4	2	2.00	0.39
P. radius	9	2	4.50	0.42
D. radius	3	2	1.50	0.43
P. ulna	1	2	0.50	0.30
D. ulna	0	2	0	0.44
P. metacarpal	1	2	0.50	0.56
D. metacarpal	0	2	0	0.49
P. femur	1	2	0.50	0.36
D. femur	2	2	1.00	0.28
P. tibia	3	2	1.50	0.30
D. tibia	11	2	5.50	0.50
Tarsal	2	10	0.20	0.39
Astragalus	3	2	1.50	0.47
Calcaneus	5	2	2.50	0.64
P. metatarsal	4	2	2.00	0.55
D. metatarsal	0	2	0	0.46
Phalanx I	10	8	1.25	0.42
Phalanx II	6	8	0.75	0.25
Phalanx III	2	8	0.25	0.25

[1] Minimum anatomical units
[2] From Lyman (1985)

Four major questions about the subsistence economy
of subsidiary centers can be addressed with faunal data:

1. Did different components of the chiefdom use, or
   have direct access to, grossly different sets or mix-
   tures of faunal resources?

2. Is there evidence of any net movement of meat into or out of subsidiary centers?

3. What do the faunal remains indicate about the abundance of local fauna?

4. What do the faunal remains indicate about the extent of human modification of the local environment?

Overall Faunal Procurement

A prominent aspect of the redistributive model of chiefdom economies is the postulation that disjunct distributions of resources require a mechanism for their redistribution. Correlatively, the catchments of sites in a chiefdom are expected to differ significantly. Earle (1977, 1978) showed that this was *not* the case on the Hawaiian island of Kaua'i, but it is an open question whether this is generally true of chiefdoms. In the present case, components of the Moundville III phase are in very similar ecological settings. All subsidiary centers are on terrace-levees within 0.5 km of the river or on a large oxbow lake. Residents at these sites, as well as residents of nearby farmsteads, would thus have had immediate access to the same basic set of faunal resources. That the available resources were actually exploited in the same proportions at each of the sites is an issue best resolved by examining faunal remains from each of the sites. Since this is not currently possible, a less direct approach is necessary.

In table 4.2, the White site fauna is compared with fauna from several nearby Mississippian sites. Percentages by weight of identified fauna are used to eliminate the biasing effect of differential fragmentation of bone at the various sites. All data represent material from ¼-in. mesh waterscreen, except for the Moundville sample, which is from flotation samples (effectively ¹⁄₁₆-in. mesh screen). The comparative data come from Moundville and from sites along the central Tombigbee River, 45 to 70 km northwest of the White site. Yarborough is a single-dwelling farmstead. Lubbub is a local chiefdom center, the apex of a two-level settlement hierarchy.

The principal feature of the data in table 4.2 is the overall similarity between sites. The proportions of faunal classes consumed are roughly the same, regardless of the position of sites in their settlement hierarchy. While the similarity of physiographic settings and of general consumption patterns may seem to be *prima facie* evidence against the redistribution model, the situation is actually much more complicated. The most important complication is that the similar overall consumption patterns might actually be the *result* of highly effective redistribution of faunal resources. Conceivably, despite similar settings, individual communities may have specialized in procuring restricted sets of fauna, but redistribution of these foods provided all communities with equal proportions for consumption. There are two reasons to believe this is not the case, both of them relating to the distance between sites.

First, we must keep in mind that bones are actually the by-products of both preparation and consumption of meat. If the similarities in table 4.2 are the result of efficient redistribution, then *bones* were being redistributed as well as meat. The straight-line distance between the northernmost and southernmost contemporary subsidiary sites of the Moundville chiefdom is 30 km; the sites are 70 km apart along the river. If meat were being moved in quantity between sites, movement of the entire skeleton as well as the meat would entail a considerable waste of energy. Most likely, at least some portions of the skeleton would be removed before transport in order to reduce the load weight. By extension, if sites were specialized in procuring different sets of fauna, we would not expect the weight of bones of any

Table 4.2 Comparison of White Site Faunal Data with
Fauna from Nearby Mississippian Sites

Site (Component)		% of identified		
	Large mammal	Small mammal	Bird	Turtle
White site (late Moundville III)[1]	82.3	3.4	3.5	9.4
Moundville (Moundville I)[2]	84.7	6.1	5.9	trace
Yarborough (Protohistoric)[3]	73.7	6.4	4.6	13.3
Lubbub (Protohistoric)[3]	83.4	4.3	8.4	2.9
Lubbub (Summerville II/III)[3]	83.4	4.1	7.1	0.1
Lubbub (Summerville I)[3]	84.5	4.6	6.2	3.9

[1] Michals, unpublished data
[2] From Scott (1982, tables 54, 56)
[3] From Scott (1983, appendix B)
[4] Weight not available

given taxon to be similar at all sites. At the least, sites should differ markedly in the abundance of specific body parts of a given taxon. I show later in this chapter that sites do differ in the proportion of deer body parts. The differences, however, do not appear to be related to preparation of venison for transport.

There is a second reason that the distance between sites renders transportation of entire skeletons improbable. In the hot, humid Alabama summer, meat spoils rapidly. Transportation of meat to and from the redistribution center would take considerable time, in many cases longer than fresh meat would remain edible, even by aboriginal standards. At least during the summer, meat would likely have been dried before transportation. In the drying process, most of the bones

bone by weight			Total weight identified (g)	Weight unidentified (g)
Snake	Amphibian	Fish		
0.4	trace	1.0	2,595.1	1,010.1
--[4]	--	3.2	871.0	206.1
0.9	0.2	1.0	11,887.9	1,118.1
0.2	0.1	0.8	4,738.4	411.8
0.1	0.1	0.6	4,371.5	319.3
0.1	0.1	0.7	783.0	106.4

would be discarded (Swanton 1946, 373–78). For example, Catesby ([1731–43] quoted in Swanton 1946, 374) described meat-drying he saw in the Carolina-to-Florida area:

> Besides roasting and boiling, they barbecue most of the flesh of the larger animals, such as buffalo's [sic], bear and deer: this is performed very gradually, over a slow clear fire, upon a large wooden gridiron, raised two feet above the fire. By this method of curing venison it will keep good five or six weeks, and by its being divested of the bone, and cut into portable pieces, adapts it to their use, for the more easy conveyance of it. . . . Fish is also thus preserved. . . .

Again anticipating a later section of this chapter, the different relative porportions of deer body parts at different sites do not appear to stem from specialization in procuring and drying venison.

Despite the overall similarity of faunal proportions shown in table 4.2, some differences deserve comment. The Yarborough site had a relatively low proportion of deer bone, which Scott (1982, 149–50) attributes to abandonment of the site for intensive deer hunting during November and December. The Lubbub site, in contrast, *was* occupied during this season, and much of the skeleton of deer procured then was deposited at the site. Yarborough also had relatively large amounts of turtle, snake, and amphibian bones. Scott argues that this is not simply the effect of seasonal abandonment of the site. She notes (1983, 150) that the *number* of turtle, snake, and amphibian bones at Yarborough was roughly four, six, and five times higher, respectively, than in the combined Lubbub sample, despite similar overall sample sizes. Scott's conclusion is that hunting was more important at the Yarborough farmstead than at the Lubbub village. The White site is intermediate between Lubbub and Yarborough in faunal composition, with less amphibian bone than either site and intermediate abundances of turtle and snake. By these criteria, the Moundville fauna seems to indicate a low emphasis on hunting. The Moundville sample, however, is so small that little importance can be attached to differences of a few percentage points.

Several factors besides the small size of the Moundville sample complicate these intersite comparisons. It would be helpful to compare bone counts and meat-weight contributions estimated from minimum-number-of-individual (MNI) values. These data are available for Lubbub and Yarborough (Scott 1983, appendix B; 1982, table 54), but bone counts are not available for Moundville nonmammalian fauna, and MNI values are not available for most nonmammalian fauna from Moundville and White.

The available MNI values for Moundville (Michals 1981) and White fauna are listed in table 4.3, along with projected meat yields. Scott's (1983, table 21) MNI-to-

meat weight conversion factors were used, unless otherwise noted. The relative dietary contributions of large
and small mammal remains at the two sites are very
close: deer contributed 88.3 percent of the mammalian
meat total at White, 92 percent in Moundville III deposits
at Moundville, and 90.7 percent in Moundville I samples
at Moundville. There is variation within the small mammal category. Beaver and raccoon contributed most of
the small mammal meat at White, yet neither was identified in the Moundville samples. Instead, canids contributed most of the small mammal meat in the Moundville
samples. The small mammal sample sizes are low, however, so these contrasts should be interpreted with caution. Though the avian fauna from White was not
systematically identified, wild turkey and at least one
teal-size bird are known to be present. Their inclusion in
the meat contribution column in table 4.3 would bring
the overall large mammal/small mammal/bird percentages into even closer alignment with the Moundville
percentages.

Another factor to be borne in mind is that the Moundville sample comes from one area at the north end of the
site. Judging from its location and associated artifacts,
this area was not a residential precinct for "commoners"
(Scarry 1986), though precisely what status the residents had is not entirely clear. Since faunal remains
were not systematically collected during the extensive,
earlier excavations elsewhere at the site, it is not clear
whether the provenience of the available sample biases
its content.

There are yet other difficulties with the intersite comparisons presented here. For instance, Michals calculated Moundville MNI values by summing MNI values
per feature, while I calculated MNI values for the White
site by summing without regard for horizontal or vertical location. The highly stratified nature of the deposits at Moundville, as opposed to the partially mixed

Table 4.3 Faunal MNI Values and Meat Weight Contributions from the White and Moundville Sites

Species	Moundville[1] (Moundville I)			White (Moundville III)		
	MNI	Projected meat yield (kg)	% of total meat yield	MNI	Projected meat yield (kg)	% of total meat yield
White-tailed deer	13	370.5	85.8	7	199.5	88.1
Gray squirrel	11	3.85	0.9	1	0.35	0.2
Fox squirrel	2	1.12	0.3	0	0	0
Indeterminate squirrel	0	0	0	1	0.45[2]	0.2
Swamp rabbit	2	2.0	0.5	1	1.0	0.4
Cottontail rabbit	4	2.0	0.5	1	0.5	0.2
Indeterminate rabbit	0	0	0	1	0.75[3]	0.3
Opossum	1	1.4	0.3	1	1.4	0.6
Raccoon	0	0	0	2	5.2	2.3
Domestic dog	2	7.2	1.7	0	0	0
Gray wolf	1	13.64	3.2	0	0	0

	MNI	Meat	%	MNI	Meat	%
Coyote	1	6.9[5]	1.6	0	0	0
Fox (red ?)	0	0	0	1	1.8[6]	0.8
Indeterminate canid	0	0	0	1	3.6[7]	1.6
Beaver	0	0	0	1[8]	11.8	5.2
Wild turkey	6	23.1	5.4	-[8]	-	-
Indeterminate snake	11	-[9]	-	-[8]	-	-
Indeterminate turtle	4	-[9]	-	-[8]	-	-
Total	58	431.67	100.2	18	225.99	99.9

1 MNI values from Michals (1981, 92); meat yields for these and White site MNI values calculated using conversion factors in Scott (1983, table 21)

2 Calculated using unweighted average of gray and fox squirrel meat yield values

3 Calculated using unweighted average of cottontail and swamp rabbit meat yield values

4 Meat yield value from Smith (1975, 173)

5 Meat yield value from Gipson (1978, 199); his average live weight values modified to eliminate red wolf hybrids, and assuming usable meat yield of 50% of live weight

6 Calculated using value for gray fox

7 Calculated using value for domestic dog

8 Present but MNI not calculated

9 Present but not necessarily eaten, so meat yields not included in calculations

White site midden, may render this difference of approaches preferable to a (simplistically?) standardized approach, but the point is certainly debatable. Regarding comparisons between White or Moundville on the one hand, and Lubbub or Yarborough on the other, there is the problem of the presence or absence of black bear in archaeological assemblages. Archaeologists working in eastern North America have long recognized that culturally prescribed patterns of disposal of bear post-cranial remains may systematically underrepresent bear in archaeological assemblages (e.g., Parmalee et al. 1972; Smith 1975, 118–19). Thus, the presence or abundance of bear bone may have little relationship with its dietary significance. Bear was identified in the Lubbub and Yarborough samples but not in the White or Moundville samples. Elimination of bear from the Lubbub large mammal data reduces the degree of similarity between the Lubbub and White site data. A host of other problems involved in comparing these data sets can be identified. Most of them are probably of minor importance individually, though their cumulative effect may be significant. Nearly all of these problems are impossible to resolve without restudy of the original and/or new collections.

On the basis of the available data, it appears that overall faunal procurement strategies at Lubbub, White, and Moundville were similar, while there may have been greater emphasis on hunting at the Yarborough farmstead. It should be emphasized that the differences between sites are all quantitative, not qualitative. Nothing in the available data suggests specialization of hunting activities by site, contrary to the expectations derived from the redistribution model.

Provisioning

While the site locations and faunal remains do not support the redistributive model, this does not necessarily mean that the mobilization model is accurate. In addition to specifying that all components of the chiefdom be situated with equally direct access to necessary resources, the mobilization model further specifies that elite members of society be provided with subsistence goods by commoners. I use the term *provisioning* to refer to such mobilization of subsistence goods. Provisioning should be visible archaeologically as a net movement of some kinds of foods, particularly the more desirable foods, from low-status contexts of production and initial processing to high-status contexts of consumption. In a brilliantly conceived analysis, Susan Scott (1981) presented evidence of provisioning in the Mississippian period in the central Tombigbee River valley. Since her analytic approach has appeared in publications (Scott 1981, 1982, 1983, 1984) unfamiliar or unavailable to those not specializing in southeastern United States archaeology, her approach will be reviewed in some detail.

Scott's analysis was designed to determine whether different species or parts of an animal were consumed in different social contexts. She focused on the distribution of white-tailed deer remains at sites of different hierarchical levels in a two-tier Mississipian settlement pattern. Yarborough (Solis and Walling 1982) is the lower-level site, a single-structure farmstead with an associated trash dump. Lubbub (Peebles, ed., 1983a, 1983b, 1983c) is the upper-level site, a fortified village with a platform mound and central plaza. The inferred provisioning probably did not actually operate between these two sites, since there are other village-mound sites closer to Yarborough than is Lubbub. Rather, to the extent that both sites are typical of their respective site types, provisioning occurred in the broader communities of which each site was a component.

Scott's analysis, in outline, proceeded as follows. Each deer and unidentified large mammal bone was recorded separately for skeletal element, portion of the element, degree of completeness, and weight of the fragment. The bones of a complete deer skeleton were weighed to provide reference values for the relative weights to be expected if all portions of deer skeletons were discarded at an individual site. Use of bone weights rather than counts minimized the effects of between-site differences in degree of fragmentation. To further control for the effects of differential fragmentation, unidentified large mammal bone fragments—which, in the southeastern United States, are most likely overwhelmingly deer bone fragments too incomplete to identify—were classified either as long bone fragments or as other unidentified fragments. Thus, at a gross level, the highly fragmented unidentified large mammal fragments could be compared to the relative abundances of identified elements to determine whether long bones (or other parts of the skeleton) could be "hidden" in the unidentified fragments. The relative abundances of skeletal parts at the two sites were then compared to determine whether they differed from the reference values or from each other.

Scott's (1981) comparison of the data from the two sites showed that:

> [when] the relative frequencies of white-tailed deer skeletal elements in the two assemblages are compared, a pattern emerges which strongly suggests that ceremonial centers were provisioned to some extent by outlying settlements. . . . What is different about the two assemblages is how well represented the heavily muscled elements are. Most of the meat on white-tailed deer is obtained from the upper limbs, which are far better represented in the Lubbub Creek assemblage. In contrast, bones of the skull and feet which produce little or no meat are far more common in the Yarborough site sample.

Scott was also able to show that the more extensive fragmentation of bones at Yarborough was not the cause of the discrepancy, since even among the unidentified large mammal remains, Lubbub had an appreciably higher relative weight of long bone shafts than Yarborough.

The White site faunal remains were analyzed by Scott's technique. Before the results are presented, an additional issue must be discussed. In the area of the Lubbub and Yarborough sites in the Mississippian period, there was a two-level site hierarchy, namely, the local centers with one or more mounds and the dispersed farmsteads. The Moundville area had a three-level site hierarchy: the multimound Moundville site, single-mound subsidiary centers such as White, and dispersed farmsteads. Clearly, we would expect the elite at Moundville to be provisioned. We would also expect the elite residents at the subsidiary sites to be provisioned. In the tribute model, however, subsidiary centers also collect or produce goods to be passed upward to the paramount elites. Therefore, would we expect the White site overall to have a provisioned or a provisioning faunal assemblage?

The answer depends on several factors. One factor is whether (and what proportion of) meaty cuts of deer were among the goods passed upward from the White site. Another factor is whether dismemberment of deer carcasses took place before or after deer meat was brought to the White site. I see no a priori basis for resolving either issue. Consequently, the results of the analysis may be ambiguous. If the deer assemblage is enriched in meaty cuts, we can assume the local elite was provisioned. If the assemblage is enriched in meat-poor cuts, or if there is no net enrichment of any body part, we cannot conclude that the local elite were *not* provisioned until data from farmsteads and from Moundville are available for a more complete determination of the spatial patterning of deer dismemberment and body part transport. As it turns out, the body part data indicate an enrichment of meaty body parts at the White site.

Table 4.4 Proportions of Deer Body Parts at White, Lubbub (Summerville I–IV), and Yarborough

| Body part | % of identified elements by weight | | | | |
	Control deer[1]	White	Lubbub[2]	Yarborough[2]	Lubbub-Yarborough average
Skull	11.9	6.7	16.7	26.3	21.5
Axial	25.5	21.3	15.1	7.9	11.5
Forelimb	17.2	9.1	22.9	10.8	16.9
Hind limb	26.8	41.0	30.2	13.0	21.6
Foot	18.9	21.9	15.2	42.0	28.6

[1] Proportions from a single buck, aged ca. 14 months; total weight of skeleton = 2573.4 g (Scott 1983, 355)
[2] From Scott (1982, table 52)

The deer body part data for the White, Lubbub, and Yarborough sites are presented in table 4.4 but are most easily comprehended by looking at figure 4.2. Both the Lubbub and White data more closely resemble the complete deer profile than do the Yarborough data. The Lubbub and White profiles, however, are quite different. Each resembles the complete deer more closely than they resemble each other (Brainerd-Robinson coefficients: White-deer = 165.3; Lubbub-deer = 172; White-Lubbub = 152.5). Lubbub has higher than expected values for skull, forelimb, and hind limb, while White has higher than expected values for hind limb and feet. This suggests that the White site elite were provisioned with hind limbs only, instead of both forelimbs and hind limbs, as was the case at Lubbub. A note of caution is appropriate here: bones from some parts of deer that were consumed at the site might have been deposited somewhere other than the 4-x-6-m area that yielded the present sample. Since there is no evidence of preserved faunal remains elsewhere at the site, the issue cannot easily be resolved.

Though the sample is too small to permit a rigorous

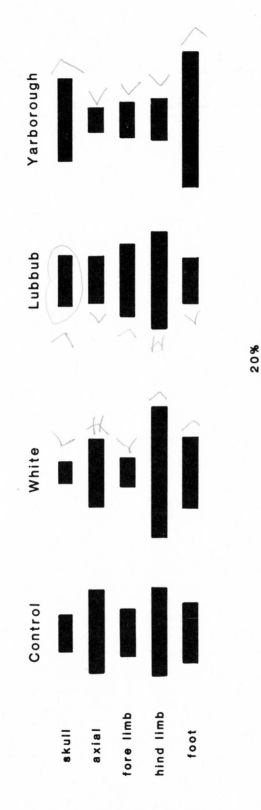

Figure 4.2 Comparison of Deer Body Parts from the White, Lubbub, and Yarborough Sites

Table 4.5 Frequencies of Deer Axial Skele-
ton Elements, White Site (late
Moundville III) and Moundville
(Moundville I)

Element	No. of fragments White	Moundville[1]
Vertebrae (total)	45	18
Cervical	4	0
Thoracic	3	8
Lumbar	11	8
Indeterminate	27	2
Rib fragments	36	21
Sternum	1	0
Pelvis (total)	9	4
Sacrum	0	1
Ilium	1 (1R)	2
Ischium	4 (3L,1R)	1
Pubis	2 (1R,1?)	0
Cf. innominate	2	0

[1] L. Michals, personal communication

analysis, the differential abundance of bones of the axial skeleton suggests that the White site was provisioned with the entire posterior halves of deer, not just the hind limbs. Table 4.5 presents the counts and weights of the axial skeletal fragments. Lumbar vertebral fragments are more numerous than those of cervical or thoracic vertebrae, even though both cervical and thoracic vertebrae outnumber lumbar vertebrae in a normal deer. Gilbert (1980, 126) gives the cervical:thoracic:lumbar vertebral formula for deer as 7:13:6. To show how markedly the White site deer vertebrae data depart from this formula, we can construct a measure analogous to "percent of MNI present." In this instance, the sample is

too small and too fragmented for MNI values to be meaningful. Rather, I assume that if whole deer were being
consumed and discarded at the site, the actual number
of cervical, thoracic, and lumbar vertebral *fragments*
ought to maintain roughly the same proportionality as
the number of these three types of vertebrae in a whole
deer. By implication, I assume all vertebrae are subject
to the same degree of fragmentation. Admittedly, this
assumption may be unrealistic, though it is certainly
more justifiable than comparing counts of fragments of
grossly dissimilar skeletal elements. Taking the eleven
lumbar fragments as the baseline (i.e., 100 percent of
expected), the cervical and thoracic fragments are only
31 percent and 12.6 percent as numerous as expected,
respectively. This greater relative frequency of lumbar
vertebral fragments is paralleled by the number of pelvis
fragments (nine) relative to sternum fragments (one).
While the sternum is more likely to suffer taphonomic
loss than the pelvis, these relationships are *suggestive*
of provisioning of the White site elite with posterior
halves of deer. This conclusion is uncertain until a
larger sample size permits a more rigorous analysis.

Regardless of whether the posterior vertebrae and the
pelvis were included, it is interesting that the White site
elite were provisioned with *posterior* cuts of meat.
Bogan (1980, 44) found that forelimbs were disproportionately abundant in high-status parts of the Toqua site
in Tennessee and suggested that this was a "prestigious
cut" of the deer. Scott (1983, 354–56) compared mound-
associated and village contexts at Lubbub and found
that while both forelimbs and hind limbs were more
abundant in mound context than in village context, the
abundance of forelimbs was much more enhanced in
mound context than that of hind limbs. It may be dan-
gerous to generalize from these results, but if it is true
that forelimbs were the most prestigious cut, then con-

ceivably the deficiency of forelimbs at the White site reflects the White site elite's inferior status relative to the elite at Moundville. That is, the White site elite was provisioned with meaty cuts (the hind limbs) but were themselves provisioning the higher elite with the choicest cut (the forelimbs). Admittedly, this is a post hoc interpretation. A number of other interpretations are possible, including the possibility that forelimbs were disposed of elsewhere at the White site. At the time of this writing, Lauren Michals is analyzing an expanded sample of faunal remains from Moundville for further information about the distribution of deer body parts at different communities in the Moundville chiefdom.

Table 4.5 also presents the counts of deer axial skeletal data from Moundville. The conclusion I draw from these data is that the sample is too small to be meaningful. Michals (1981, 93) listed MNI values (the sums of MNIs per feature for thirty features) for all deer elements present in her samples. She argued that the predominance of ribs and vertebrae was suggestive of removal of deer distal body parts before transportation to Moundville. Ribs and vertebrae, however, are the most numerous bones in the deer skeleton and would outnumber the distal elements even if intact carcasses were brought to the site. Again, given the very small sample, it is not possible to reach any conclusions about the shape in which deer meat was brought to Moundville.

In comparing body part data from different sites, Scott (1983) argues that it is necessary to show that differential fragmentation, and hence differential identifiability, of bones between the sites is not responsible for apparent differences in abundance of body parts. By adding the weights of identified and unidentified long bone fragments and dividing by total weight of all large mammal remains, she showed that the more fragmented Yarborough remains were still deficient in long bones

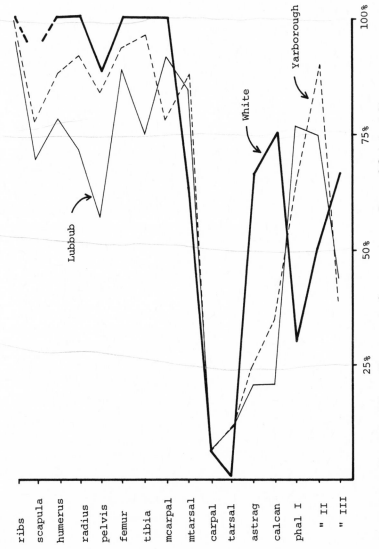

Figure 4.3 Percent of Bone Fragments One-quarter or Less of Original Size

relative to Lubbub. Long bones represented 64 percent
of all large mammal remains at Lubbub, but only 55 percent at Yarborough. Figure 4.3 shows the percentage by
element of bones reduced to one-quarter or less of their
original size, for Lubbub, Yarborough, and White. For
most parts of the body, particularly the upper limbs and
torso, the White site remains are the most extensively
fragmented of the three. Unlike the situation at Lubbub,
where both forelimbs and hind limbs appeared overrepresented, at White the forelimbs are underrepresented, while the hind limbs are overrepresented. If
differential fragmentation is *not* responsible for this
pattern, we can predict that the overall percentage of
large mammal long bone at White should be lower than
at Lubbub and higher than at Yarborough. As shown in
table 4.6, this is in fact the case, confirming that bone
fragmentation is not responsible for the pattern of relative body part abundances.

Abundance of Local Fauna

The seasonality of deer hunting and the age structure
of the procured deer were examined, using dental age
estimates provided by Susan Scott. The deer dental remains, unfortunately, reveal little about the seasonality
of deer procurement. Estimation of deer age by dental
wear and eruption patterns is most reliable when entire
tooth rows are preserved intact. Most of the deer teeth in
unmixed, above-floor contexts at White were isolated
teeth. Consequently, the age ranges estimated for most
of the teeth are too broad to be useful in determining
season of death. One excavation unit contained three
right deciduous premolars, which, if they came from a
single individual, indicate an age at death of around ten
weeks. Assuming an average birth date of 1 August (cf.
Scott 1982, 150), this fawn probably died around the be-

Table 4.6 Large Mammal Body Part Data for White, Lubbub, and Yarborough

Body part	% of all large mammal bone by weight[1] White	Lubbub[1]	Yarborough[1]
Forelimb	4.7	13.9	5.1
Hind limb	21.3	18.3	6.1
Unidentified large mammal long bone	37.7	31.8	43.6
Total long bone	63.7	64.0	54.8
Skull	3.5	10.1	12.3
Axial	11.1	9.2	3.7
Foot	11.4	9.2	19.6
Unidentified large mammal	10.3	7.6	9.7
Total other bone	36.3	36.1	45.3
Total weight of large mammal bone	2,137.8 g	14,662.6 g	8,678.0 g

[1] From Scott (1982, Table 52); totals do not include identified bear bone.

ginning of November. None of the other teeth can be assigned a range for age at death of less than six months. When a range this large is added to the dispersion of actual birth dates around the 1 August average, no reliable information on season of kill can be extracted.

The estimation of deer ages revealed something else about the deer remains, however. Most of the deer teeth were from mature adults. This is shown in figure 4.4, in which the age structure of the White site deer is contrasted with that of Lubbub deer. The vertical scale in this figure is MNI for Lubbub. Since intact dentitions were rare at White, dental MNI estimates are not reliable. Instead, I have plotted the number of teeth (or partial dentitions) that may be in a given age range, e.g., a three- to five-year-old tooth (or dentition) contributes 0.5 to both the three- to four- and four- to five-year classes. The White site sample is very small, so conclusions about the age structure of the White site deer assemblage are necessarily tentative. It appears, however, that the deer from Lubbub and those from White have different age structures, with the Lubbub sample being primarily young individuals and the White sample being primarily mature adults (see figure 4.4).

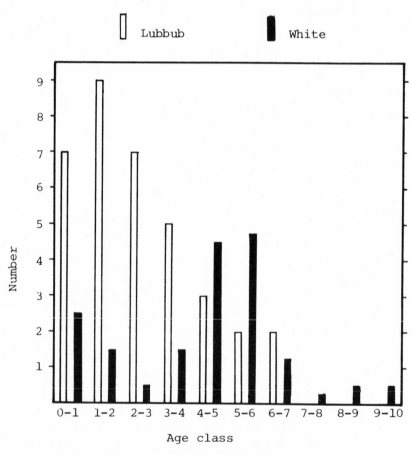

Figure 4.4 Age Distribution of White and Lubbub Deer

There are two possible reasons for the age structure of the White site deer. First, a narrow focus on prime ① adults would be a rational hunting strategy only if there were an abundance of deer. Since deer extremities are present at White in about the frequency expected for whole deer (see above), most deer at White probably were procured fairly nearby. Therefore, the age structure implies there was a local abundance of deer. However, there is another possible explanation of the age structure. Provisioning of "nobility" may have involved principally ② the prime animals taken in the hunt. I question whether such selectivity accounts for the observed age structure, since cranial remains, and the anterior half of deer generally, are less abundant at the site than expected. If the White site nobility were not getting anterior parts of deer generally, why would those anterior parts present be from prime individuals? Vagaries of sampling and preservation, of course, may be involved here, and I do not think the data are strong enough to discount the "noble gourmet" explanation.

Modification of the Local Environment

Faunal remains can provide another line of evidence on the local subsistence strategy, specifically, the extent of forest clearance near a site. The species composition of the fauna at a site should reflect the character of the local vegetation, particularly for the smaller fauna probably procured close to the site. Scott (1983, 361–63), for instance, demonstrated a shift in the Lubbub subsistence remains from forest-dwelling to brush- or field-dwelling taxa coincident with the shift from foraging/gardening to dependence on agriculture. Specifically, she argued, the ratios of gray squirrel to fox squirrel and swamp rabbit to cottontail indicated the extent of forest clearance around the site. For both pairs of species, the White site faunal assemblage is dominated by the species preferring a closed forest habitat (swamp rabbit, gray squirrel) rather than a more open or successional one (cottontail, fox squirrel; see table 4.7). This is true whether bone counts or bone weights are considered (since swamp rabbits and fox squirrels are larger than their congeners, count data should be given priority). Swamp rabbit bones are more numerous than those of cottontail (28:3) or cottontail plus indeterminate rabbit (28:6). No bones were identified as fox squirrel, and gray squirrel bones outnumber those of indeterminate squirrel (4:1). To the extent that the assumption of local procurement of small fauna is valid, these ratios indicate that the site environs were not extensively cleared for agriculture nor were they lying fallow. By implication, population density must not have been sufficiently high to create a shortage of agricultural land.

As the reader may expect, however, there is a complicating factor. At Lubbub, most of the land surround-

Table 4.7 Counts and Weights of Identified Small Mammal Bones, White Site

Species	Count		Weight	
	no.	%	g	%
Canis sp.	11	13.9	20.06	39.7
Swamp rabbit	28	35.4	9.04	17.9
Cottontail rabbit	3	3.8	0.96	1.9
Indeterminate rabbit	3	3.8	0.42	0.8
Opossum	13	16.5	7.82	15.5
Raccoon	12	15.2	5.56	11.0
Beaver	1	1.3	1.61	3.2
Gray squirrel	4	5.1	1.55	3.1
Indeterminate squirrel	1	1.3	0.17	0.3
Fox	2	2.5	3.27	6.5
Rodent	1	1.3	0.04	<0.1
Total	79	100.1	50.05	99.9

ing the site was fairly well drained and the soils were
medium textured. It would be suitable land for cultivation with aboriginal technology. At White, most of the
soils near the site are poorly drained and clayey. The
land probably would not have been cleared for fields,
even if there were a local shortage of agricultural land.
Hence the White site squirrel and rabbit ratios would
have been informative if the *field*-preferring species pre-
dominated. The predominance of *forest*-preferring species reveals only that land shortage was not so severe
that the populace was trying to farm the backswamp.

Summary

The four questions posed of the faunal remains have
been answered with varying degrees of success. First,
current data suggest that all sites of the Moundville
chiefdom had direct access to the same overall set of
faunal resources and exploited them in a fundamentally
similar way. Larger samples, further quantification of
available samples, and samples from additional sites are
necessary to add confidence to this conclusion. Second,
there is strong evidence for provisioning of the elite residents at the White subsidiary center. These elite members of society preferentially received meaty posterior
portions of white-tailed deer, though the distribution
pattern for the rest of the carcass is not yet known.
Third, the age structure of the deer at White suggests an
abundance of local fauna, though postkill selection of
deer for transport to White cannot be ruled out as the
cause of the age structure's shape. Fourth, the species
composition of the small mammal remains does not reveal any *severe* shortage of agricultural land, but the
small mammal remains are expected to be a relatively
insensitive indicator of such shortage.

Plant Exploitation

The patterns of production and distribution of plant resources in the Moundville chiefdom can be examined through a combination of catchment analyses and study of the botanical remains from the White site. Site catchment data have already been studied by Peebles (1978a) and Bozeman (1982), though with different aims. The analysis of botanical remains from White focuses on material from the late Moundville III refuse deposit.

Three issues about the subsistence economy of the chiefdom are examined below:

1. Did all communities of the chiefdom have similarly direct access to wild botanical resources?

2. Were all communities at locations with similar potential agricultural productivity?

3. What was the pattern of plant utilization at White, and is this consistent with the expectations derived from the catchment analysis?

Site Catchments: Wild Plant Resources

The location of the Moundville chiefdom with respect to regional phytogeography is presented in chapter three. An important point in that discussion is that, while several substantially different vegetation associations (e.g., Black Belt prairies, Cumberland Plateau mixed mesophytic forests) occur *near* the sites of the Moundville chiefdom, *all* of the sites are on the Black Warrior River floodplain. Thus some sites are closer to the Fall Line Hills forests and others are closer to the Black Belt, but all of the sites are in grossly similar settings. There is one important exception to this statement. Moundville itself sits on a high terrace at the edge of the floodplain, with the river on one side and the Fall Line Hills on the other. Generally, however, there is no major phytogeographic difference between sites of the chiefdom, such as the redistribution model would suggest.

The overall similarity of the locations of the subsidiary sites can be seen at a finer scale by looking at the distribution of soil types nearby. Bozeman (1982, 284) lists the area of each of fifteen soil types found within a 1-km walk from each site (it is assumed that catchments did not cross substantial bodies of water, unless the far side could be reached by a 1-km walk around the margins). These soil types can be grouped into five classes on the basis of drainage characteristics (Rowe et al. 1912; Winston et al. 1914), which largely determine the vegetation naturally occurring on them. The soil type groupings are listed in table 4.8. The proportional representation of these groups by catchment is presented in table 4.9. Only sites occupied during Moundville III are listed in this table, in order to avoid comparison between sites occupied during different stages in the growth of the Moundville chiefdom. Five of the six sites are surrounded by moderately well drained soils, with variation in the frequency of flooding. The sixth site, White, contrasts sharply with the other five because most of its catchment is poorly drained. To determine whether this constitutes partial support for the redistribution model, the significance of the contrast must be examined more closely.

The data in table 4.9 come from soil surveys performed early in this century (Rowe et al. 1912; Winston et al. 1914). The coarse grain of the mapping probably exaggerates the differences between sites. Though more recent soil surveys exist for the two relevant counties (Edwards et al. 1939; Johnson 1981), they are not comparable either in the soil types distinguished or in the level of mapping detail. Nevertheless, the 1-km radius

Table 4.8 Grouping of Soil Types by Drainage Characteristics[1]

Poorly drained, frequently flooded	Moderate drainage, regularly flooded	Moderate to good drainage, rarely flooded	Moderate to good drainage, level or rolling uplands	Well drained, steep uplands
Waverly clay loam	Huntington silty loam	Cahaba sandy loam	Greenville loam	Guin gravelly sandy loam
Bibb fine silty loam	Cahaba silty loam	Cahaba fine sandy loam	Susquehanna fine sandy loam	Orangeburg gravelly sandy loam
	Ocklockonee fine sandy loam	Cahaba loam	Ruston fine sandy loam	Orangeburg fine sandy loam
		Kalmia fine sandy loam		

[1] From Rowe et al. (1912) and Winston et al. (1914)

Table 4.9 Areas of Soil Groups in 1-km Catchments for Moundville III Single-mound Sites[1]

Site	Poorly drained, frequently flooded		Moderate drainage regularly flooded		Moderate to good drainage rarely flooded		Moderate to good drainage, level or rolling uplands		Well drained steep uplands	
	ha	%	ha	%	ha	%	ha	%	ha	%
1Tu2/3	0	0	365	80	15	3	55	12	20	4
1Tu46/47	0	0	235	50	235	50	0	0	0	0
1Tu42/43	0	0	0	0	403	100	0	0	0	0
1Ha14/15	159[2]	29	0	0	382	71	0	0	0	0
1Ha107A	26	5	0	0	499	95	0	0	0	0
1Ha7/8	516	92	0	0	43	8	0	0	0	0

1 Adapted from Bozeman (1982, 284)
2 Area of Cahaba clay loam listed by Bozeman (1982, 284) was a typographical error; value used here is correct.

catchment of the White site definitely is relatively more flood-prone and less well drained than the other Moundville III site catchments. It is thus expected to have had different proportions of naturally occurring vegetal resources.

The composition of Black Warrior floodplain forest communities has been studied by Margaret Scarry (1986). She identified three physiographic settings on the floodplain (riverbank, swamp, and bottomland) and tallied General Land Office (GLO) witness tree counts for each setting. The GLO surveys were conducted from 1819 to 1821, which was before Euro-American settlement in the area significantly altered the local forest composition, and after a 140-year hiatus in Native American occupation of the area (Knight 1982, 37–77; Curren 1984, 238–39; Scarry 1986). Thus the reconstructed vegetation represents what would be found with minimal anthropogenic disturbance. Information from Scarry's forest reconstruction is presented in table 4.10.

The White site would have had significantly more Swamp forest nearby than did the other Moundville III sites. In terms of economically important species, this equates to a relative scarcity of nuts and fruits. The White site catchment would have had relatively low acorn abundances, despite the higher overall proportion of oaks in Swamp forest than in Bottomland forest. Most oaks in Swamp forest are red oaks, which generally have bitter acorns. Though the responsible tannins can be leached out, it is a time-consuming process, which is not mentioned in any of the early European descriptions of aboriginal nut utilization in the Southeast (Swanton 1946, 346–47). The same point applies to hickory nut abundances. Not only are hickories less abundant in Swamp than in Bottomland forest, but relatively more of the Swamp hickories would have been bitternut and

Table 4.10 Composition of Naturally Occurring Moundville Area Forests[1]

Bottomlands		Swamp		Riverbank	
Tree	% of trees counted	Tree	% of trees counted	Tree	% of trees counted
The ten most common trees					
Holly	11.01	Holly	11.11	Maple	21.22
Sweet gum	9.78	Sweet gum	10.18	Ash	11.42
Beech	9.68	Willow oak	9.25	Hackberry	10.61
White oak	9.47	Black gum	8.79	Sycamore	8.97
Pine	7.10	White oak	7.40	Beech	6.53
Red oak	5.66	Beech	7.40	Hickory	4.89
Maple	5.45	Maple	6.94	Sweet gum	4.89
Hickory	4.73	Ash	5.09	Elm	4.48
Black gum	3.91	Cypress	4.16	Mulberry	4.48
Bay	3.50	Hornbeam	3.70	Sassafras	4.48
Food-producing trees					
Hickory	4.73	Hickory	2.77	Hickory	4.89
White oaks	11.63	White oaks	7.86	White oaks	0.81
Red oaks	11.30	Red oaks	17.56	Red oaks	2.43
Chestnut	0.51	Chestnut	0	Chestnut	0
Walnut	0.10	Walnut	0	Walnut	0
Hazel	0.10	Hazel	0	Hazel	0
Persimmon	0.72	Persimmon	0.46	Persimmon	0
Mulberry	1.23	Mulberry	2.31	Mulberry	4.48
Cherry	0.10	Cherry	0	Cherry	0
Pawpaw	0.10	Pawpaw	0	Pawpaw	0
Haw	0	Haw	0.46	Haw	0
Hackberry	0.41	Hackberry	0	Hackberry	0

[1] From Scarry (1986)

water hickories (*Carya cordiformis* and *C. aquatica*, respectively), which have bitter nuts.

Though nuts were likely the most important wild botanical resource, most other economically important plant species are not climax forest species. Most edible fruits, berries, seeds, greens, and tubers used by south-eastern Indians are successional species (Swanton 1946, 265–97; Jackson 1986, 162–200). Their abundance would be greatly increased over natural levels by creating forest edges with field clearance and by allowing cleared fields to lie fallow. Since details of the extent and distribution of fields around Moundville III sites are not known, it is impossible to compare site catchments in terms of the abundance of these resources. The relatively large proportion of permanently wet and/or not-easily-tilled soils around the White site suggests that there might have been a higher ratio of forest area to field area around this site than around its contemporaries.

Some indication of the degree of forest disturbance around the White site is provided by the wood charcoal in the late Moundville III refuse deposit. Extensive fragmentation of the charcoal resulted in low numbers of identifiable pieces. Charcoal from two flotation samples and one ¼-in. waterscreen sample were identified by Margaret Scarry (see table 4.11; five additional flotation samples were examined but had too little charcoal for reliable quantitative analysis). The predominance of pine in the wood charcoal is striking in light of the low number of pines expected for the vicinity of the site. In Scarry's (1986) forest reconstruction, only 7.10 percent and 0.46 percent, respectively, of Bottomland and Swamp forests were pines. Since pine abundance in the region around Moundville is related to the frequency of forest fires (Harper 1943, 127–50), the high proportion of pine charcoal in the late Moundville III refuse deposit at White may indicate that uncleared forests around the site were fired often. Pine is also a successful colonizer of old fields, hence the abundance of pine charcoal could also indicate the presence of extensive fallow fields around the site. Larger samples and sampling of additional contexts at the site are desirable before great certainty can be attached to these interpretations. Nev-

Table 4.11 Identified Wood Charcoal from Late Moundville III Refuse Deposit, White Site

Taxa	Flotation samples no.	Flotation samples %	1/4-in. waterscreen no.	1/4-in. waterscreen %	Total no.	Total %
Acer (maple)	1	2.5	0	0	1	1.7
Carya (hickory)	1	3.5	0	0	1	1.7
Diospyros (persimmon)	0	0	1	5.0	1	1.7
Fraxinus (ash)	0	0	1	5.0	1	1.7
Liquidambar (sweet gum)	1	2.5	1	5.0	2	3.4
Pinus (pine)	30	76.9	14	70.0	44	74.6
Quercus						
red oak	0	0	2	10.0	2	3.4
white oak	3	7.7	0	0	3	5.1
Ulmus (elm)	0	0	1	5.0	1	1.7
Zea mays (maize stalk)	3	7.7	0	0	3	5.1
Total	39	99.8	20	100.0	59	100.1

ertheless, the pine charcoal abundance contrasts strikingly with the expected background of oaks, elm, ash, sweet gum, black gum, etc.

Charred seeds in the late Moundville III refuse deposit could provide further information about the alteration of natural vegetation associations near the site. Unfortunately, however, the number of seeds in the analyzed samples is too small to be very informative. Table 4.12 lists the carbonized seeds recovered from six flotation samples (a seventh flotation sample was examined but contained no carbonized seeds). Sorting and identification were performed by Margaret Scarry. Two of the flotation samples (6 l each) were from the late Moundville III refuse deposit (164N/105E L.2 and 3). The other four were 100-percent samples of thin lenses, which composed the intact structure floor in 164N/107E. Total volume of these four samples was 9.75 l. Data for the individual samples may be found in Welch (1986, appendix C).

Table 4.12 Carbonized Seeds from Late Moundville III Refuse and Floor Contexts, White Site

Taxa	Refuse deposit (2 samples, 12 l total)	Floor deposit (4 samples, 9.75 l total)
Amaranthus (pigweed)	0	1
Celtis (hackberry)	0	2[1]
Chenopodium (goosefoot)	0	1
Compositae (composites)	0	1
Diospyros (persimmon)	35	119
Galium (bedstraw)	0	1
Ilex cf. *verticilliata* (winterberry)	2	2
Ilex cf. *vomitoria* (yaupon)	1	0
Oxalis (wood sorrel)	1	1
Passiflora (maypop)	1	5
Phalaris (maygrass)	3	4
Phytolacca (pokeweed)	4	0
Poaceae (grasses)		
Unknown type 1	5	77
Unknown type 2	3	41
Polygonum (knotweed)	0	3
Portulaca (purslane)	0	1
Rhus (sumac)	1	0
Vitis (grape)	1	1
Total identified	57	258
Total unidentified	1	3
Unidentifiable	27	74

[1] Not carbonized but included here because Lopinott (1984) argues that *Celtis* seeds may preserve without carbonization

There are generally low numbers of items per taxon, with two exceptions. One of these exceptions, the count of persimmon seed, is largely spurious. Most of the other items in the table represent whole seeds, while the entries for persimmon are counts of seed fragments. Persimmon seeds being relatively large and easily identified even when fragmented, the persimmon counts should not be directly compared to the other seed counts (M. Scarry, personal communication).

The other exception to the generally low seed counts is grass seed (Poaceae) in the floor deposits. Two distinct types are represented, with seventy-seven specimens of type 1 and forty-one specimens of type 2. Scarry was unable to identify these grasses, but they definitely are not maygrass, little barley, or fescue. Several different processes might account for the high incidence of charred grass seeds in the floor sediments. Since the sediments are ashy, perhaps the seeds are part of a generalized spread of hearth ash. Another possibility is that parts of the structure caught fire from time to time—the floor is oxidized in places—and charred seeds from roof thatch or floor matting became incorporated in the floor when the structure was refurbished. Or perhaps these seeds are by-products of intentional collection and parching of grass seeds. Without more complete information about the function(s) of the structure or the taxonomy of the seeds, it is impossible to eliminate any of these alternatives. The high incidence of these seeds is not replicated in any of the large number of floor deposits Scarry has sampled at Moundville, nor am I aware of any comparable data from Mississippian floors elsewhere in the Southeast.

One final note is necessary before turning to the agricultural side of subsistence. One holly seed from the late Moundville III refuse deposit is *tentatively* identified as *Ilex vomitoria*, the yaupon holly. Yaupon was the basis of the "black drink," an important, ceremonially consumed tea widely noted by early European observers in the Southeast (see Merrill 1979; Fairbanks 1979). Harper (1944, 148–49; Harper in Jones n.d.) found specimens of yaupon growing at Moundville. Noting that yaupon rarely occurs naturally far from the sea coast, he speculated that yaupon had been transplanted to Moundville prehistorically so that a local source would be available to the occupants of the large Moundville site. Distribution data summarized by Merrill (1979, map 1) reaffirm the primarily coastal distribution of the shrub, though the number of examples found well away from the coast leave it a moot point whether yaupon might occur naturally in the Moundville area. The shrub prefers "the harsh life of the semi-xeric conditions of the seashore and is adapted to a far lesser extent for the sterile bluffs on inland rivers" (Hu 1979, 10). While the high river bluffs at Moundville might well have supported a natural population of yaupon (two seeds are tentatively identified from Moundville I deposits at Moundville [M. Scarry, personal communication]), the wetter character of the White site suggests that the plant likely would not grow there without human intervention. On the other hand, the seed could have been introduced to the site along with yaupon leaves brought from coastal areas. Yaupon berries grow close to the stem, and if the leaves were harvested by stripping them from the stems, the berries might well have been removed with the leaves. There is no way to tell whether the possible yaupon seed from the White site came from a locally cultivated plant or not.

The data on wild plant resources do not in themselves allow us to determine the economic strategy(ies) employed by the occupants of the White site or the chiefdom at large. What these data do reveal, however, is that the locations of single-mound sites of the Moundville chiefdom were not chosen to optimize access to any (currently known) wild botanical economic resource.

Site Catchments: Agricultural Resources

Maize was the staple food of Mississippian populations, as evidenced by the accounts of early European explorers (Swanton 1946, 304–10), by the large amounts of maize recovered from Mississippian archaeological sites (Yarnell and Black 1985, 103), and by the carbon isotope composition of the bones of Mississippian people (Broida 1984; Rose and Marks 1985; Boutton et al. 1986). As with any agriculture-dependent population, a basic measure of the economic self-sufficiency of a community is its ability to produce enough of the staple crop for its own consumption. In its most extreme form, however, the redistribution model stipulates that a chiefdom integrates communities that are so ecologically disparate that staple foods would have to be imported to some of the communities. The mobilization model, in contrast, posits that chiefdoms typically are composed of self-sufficient communities. In comparing these models, therefore, it is important to determine whether all communities of the Moundville chiefdom could have produced sufficient maize for their own consumption.

The maize productivity of Moundville-area site catchments was examined by Peebles (1978a, 400–410). He was able to measure the maize productivity of Moundville-area soils on an interval (but not ratio) scale, using soil type-specific maize yields from the early 1900s. This was before the introduction of hybrid maize, machine plowing, and soil conservation practices. Factors beyond his control introduced a number of inaccuracies into his analysis, e.g., inaccurate site sizes, erroneous site locations, and inclusion of sites of different time periods. These inaccuracies were detected during the 1978–79 UMMA survey and testing program, and the new data were analyzed by Bozeman (1982) using Peebles's technique. In general, the size of archaeological sites of the Moundville chiefdom correlated highly with the agricultural productivity of 1-km-radius catchments around the sites. One site, 1Tu42/43, is an extreme outlier in this relationship, so much so that its inclusion in the calculations turns a strong positive correlation ($r >$ .7) to a weak negative one. Assuming population size varied linearly with site size, and excepting 1Tu42/43, all of the sites would have been equally able to support themselves. The anomalous position of 1Tu42/43, however, is not the only problem with this analysis. The other issues will be addressed after the problem of 1Tu42/43.

The 1Tu42/43 site is located across the river and about 4 km upstream from Moundville. Aside from a variety of pre-Mississippian occupations, the site dates primarily to Moundville III and possibly to the Protohistoric period as well. Herein lies one difficulty. There was an extensive burial urn cemetery immediately adjacent to the site (Curren 1984, 122–24). Though Curren states that the main area of the Protohistoric village associated with the cemetery is across an intermittent stream from 1Tu42/43, the 1978 UMMA surface collection of the latter site demonstrates that a Protohistoric component of unknown size was present there also (Bozeman 1982, 162). It may be that the difficulty of distinguishing Moundville III from Protohistoric artifacts significantly inflates the apparent Moundville III occupation size. Another problem is that the 1Tu42 mound was intentionally plowed down by the landowners in the 1950s. This activity is likely to have artificially expanded the area in which Moundville-era artifacts are distributed, hence increasing the apparent site size. Both of these factors suggest that the size used for this site in Bozeman's analysis is too large. Reduction of the site's size would bring it closer to the size:productivity ratio of the other single-mound sites. Whether these factors account entirely for the site's anomalous position cannot yet be determined.

A less obvious problem with Bozeman's analysis is the way in which catchments were measured. Both Peebles and Bozeman limited their catchments to the area that could be reached by a 1-km walk without crossing major oxbow lakes or the river. Though the known distribu-

tion of archaeological sites precludes major shifting of
the river course during the last thousand years, some
change is known to have occurred. For instance, the present Cypress Cutoff Lake, 4 to 5 km north of the White
site, was the active river channel in the early 1800s (M.
Scarry, personal communication). At several of the
Moundville-era sites, the opening or closing of one end
of a cutoff lake would have a dramatic impact on the
amount of land that would be included in the 1-km catchment. The dependence of the productivity measures on
catchment area can be seen in figure 4.5 (data in table

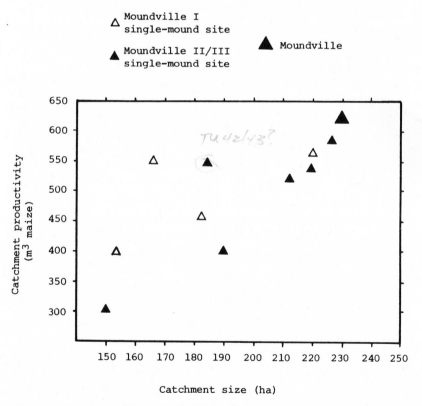

Figure 4.5 Scatterplot of Catchment Productivity versus Catchment Size, All Mound Sites

Table 4.13 Site Size and Catchment Size, Productivity, and Intrinsic Fertility for Moundville and Moundville III Single-mound Sites[1]

Site	Site size (ha)	Catchment size (ha)	productivity (m^3 maize)	intrinsic fertility (m^3 maize/ha)
Moundville	112.5	230	621	2.70
1Tu2/3	0.96	184	549	2.98
1Tu46/47	0.28	190	401	2.11
1Tu42/43	2.2	150	304	2.03
1Ha14/15	1.3	219	544	2.48
1Ha107A	0.60	212	525	2.48
1Ha7/8	0.74	226	589	2.61

[1] From Bozeman (1982)

4.13). The correlation coefficient between catchment size and productivity for all single-mound sites plus Moundville is $r = .78$ ($p < 0.01$). The correlation is even higher if only single-mound sites of Moundville III date are used in the calculation: $r = .85$ ($.05 > p > .01$). Clearly, the results of Bozeman's and Peebles's analyses are highly dependent on the twin assumptions that major bodies of water were not crossed to reach fields, and that major bodies of water were in the same locations as they are today. Redefining catchments to disregard whether water had to be crossed may sound like a reasonable way to avoid these problems, but before this analysis can be useful, we need additional information about the distribution of farmsteads across the landscape.

When Peebles conceived his site size–catchment productivity analysis, the available information indicated that most of the Moundville-era populace was nucleated at Moundville and the single-mound sites. The 1978–79 UMMA survey, however, demonstrated that the single-mound sites (except, possibly, 1Tu42/43) had relatively small resident populations. The bulk of the population outside of Moundville lived in dispersed farmsteads and small hamlets in districts or "neighborhoods" around the single-mound sites (Bozeman 1982). As yet, there is not sufficient systematic survey of the Black Warrior floodplain to determine how extensive these "neighborhoods" were. If the size of the occupation at single-mound sites is related to the productivity of the entire neighborhood rather than just the fields closest to the mound, then selection of a radius for a catchment analysis will be arbitrary and potentially misleading until there is further empirical guidance. Whether "neighborhood" productivity did in fact affect the size of the occupations around single-mound sites is a question not easy to resolve without better survey and some excavation data from the farmsteads. This does not mean, however, that all catchment analyses are potentially wrong or uninformative.

The question being asked of the catchment data is whether all sites had catchments that were equally likely to have permitted self-sufficiency in maize production. By dividing the catchment productivities by catchment size, we can remove the effect of differing catchment sizes. The resulting values are measures of intrinsic fertility of the soils near the sites. The mobilization model would predict a positive correlation between site size and intrinsic fertility, while the redistribution model does not predict any particular relationship between these two variables. Thus a strong positive correlation would be consistent with the mobilization model but would not be inconsistent with the redistribution model. The correlation between site size and catchment fertility for all Moundville III single-mound sites is low and negative ($r = -.28$, see figure 4.6). This result, however, depends on the accuracy of the size of 1Tu42/43, which is suspect. If 1Tu42/43 is omitted from the calculations, the correlation rises to r = .57. This is not statistically significant (p = .31), which is hardly surprising given the small sample size. (For this sample size, the correlation coefficient must be .88 to be significant at p = .05). The data do not contradict the expectations derived from either the mobilization or redistribution model.

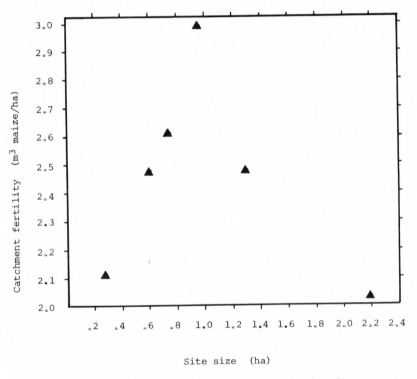

Figure 4.6 Scatterplot of Catchment Fertility and Site Size

The relationship between site size and catchment fertility for the Moundville site itself is very different from the relationship graphed in figure 4.6. Moundville's catchment fertility is higher than all but one of the Moundville III phase single-mound sites (see table 4.13), but the Moundville site is vastly larger than any of the single-mound sites. The Moundville site size listed in table 4.13 includes the area of the plaza, which was devoid of residences (Peebles 1979). Even if the area of the plaza (roughly 30 ha) is subtracted from the estimated 112-ha extent of the site, Moundville still has a qualitatively different relationship to its catchment than do the single-mound sites. Given the large size of the Moundville site, it seems highly probable that Moundville residents directly exploited a catchment of considerably larger radius than did residents of the single-mound sites. It also seems likely that the *effective* catchment of Moundville included the entire chiefdom: using Steponaitis's (1978) spatial analysis technique, Bozeman (1982, 291–301) showed that during the Moundville III phase, Moundville is nearly optimally located to receive tribute from the single-mound sites and their districts.

Maize Consumption at the White Site

The intrinsic fertility of the catchment of the White site is relatively high (see figure 4.6). This results from the frequent nutrient enrichment provided by flooding. Despite this fertility, the White site environs may have been less suitable for maize cultivation than the catchments of the other single-mound sites. As discussed above, the White site catchment is flooded more frequently than those of the other sites. Flooding frequently covers even the highest land within 1 km of the site, whereas most of the other sites are located on terrace-levees, which are flooded only sporadically. Scarry (1986) has pointed out that with aboriginal cultivation techniques, flooding is a far more likely cause of crop failure in the Black Warrior River valley than drought. Table 4.14 shows the frequency of floods by month over a seventy-seven-year interval at Tuscaloosa. Nearly 20 percent of recorded floods occurred in April or May. Another way to express these data is that thirty-nine floods occurred during April or May over a seventy-seven-year period, for an average of one flood in these months every two years. This means that most if not all of the White catchment would be inundated during the early growing season one year out of two. As Scarry (1986) noted, this would make maize cropping near the White site an unreliable mode of subsistence. Delayed planting, planting in hills, replanting after floods, and extensive aboveground storage might mitigate the effect of floods, but it can be questioned whether reliance on maize cultivated near the site would be a viable subsistence strategy.

Table 4.14 Frequency of Floods by Month at Tuscaloosa, 1888–1960[1]

Month	No. of times above flood stage	% of total number
January	36	18.2
February	39	19.7
March	55	27.8
April	27	13.6
May	12	6.1
June	2	1.0
July	3	1.5
August	0	0
September	1	0.5
October	3	1.5
November	7	3.5
December	13	6.6
Total	198	100.0

[1] From Peirce (1962, 44)

The degree of reliance on maize can be assessed from the charred plant food remains in the White site refuse deposit. Margaret Scarry analyzed the botanical material from three 6-l flotation samples from the refuse deposit and four samples (total 9.75 l) of floor deposits. The wood charcoal and seed counts are presented above (tables 4.11 and 4.12). Table 4.15 presents the data on maize and nuts. Data for individual flotation samples are presented in Welch (1986, appendix C). Due to the plethora of factors intervening between consumption of plant foods and their representation in the archaeological record (see Scarry 1986 for a review), the charred plant food data are meaningful primarily in terms of proportions relative to those found at other sites or from other times. Thus, while we cannot determine actual dietary abundances of plant foods from the charred plant remains, we can determine whether residents at White consumed more nuts and less maize than residents at other sites.

The only other archaeological plant food remains recovered from the Moundville chiefdom are from Moundville itself. Like the White site material, the Moundville material comes from flotation samples. Material from both sites was analyzed by Margaret Scarry, using identical procedures. Thus the two sets of data are fully comparable. A variety of measures could be used to examine the differences between the Moundville and White material. For example, we could compare the percentages of samples from each site that contain maize remains, or we could compare the percentages of total plant food remains that are maize (using either weight or count). The measures that I use are based on counts of pieces per liter of sample volume. Counts are used rather than weights since I compare maize remains with nutshell remains, which are much denser than maize cob fragments. The counts are divided by sample volume since the flotation samples were of various sizes. (Readers who wish to compare data presented by Scarry [1986] and those presented here should note that for most purposes Scarry standardized her sample values

Table 4.15 Counts and Weights of Maize, Nuts, and Nutshell from White Site Refuse and Floor Deposit Flotation Samples

Sample	Sample volume (1)	Plant weight (g)	Maize kernels no.	Maize kernels wt. (g)	Maize cupules no.	Maize cupules wt. (g)	Hickory shell no.	Hickory shell wt. (g)	Acorn shell no.	Acorn shell wt. (g)	Acorn meat no.	Acorn meat wt. (g)
Refuse deposit samples												
164N/105E L.1	6.0	1.52	15	0.01	26	0.06	64	0.40	7	--[1]	1	--[1]
164N/105E L.2	6.0	9.54	45	0.13	161	0.79	99	1.05	116	0.18	61	1.54
164N/105E L.3	6.0	13.74	39	0.13	107	0.31	179	1.83	350	0.58	58	0.79
Floor deposit samples												
164N/107E L.6	2.0	2.36	6	0.01	16	0.02	42	0.49	185	0.32	0	0
164N/107E L.7	1.5	3.14	3	--[1]	6	--[1]	151	1.25	127	0.18	0	0
164N/107E L.8	3.25	5.76	12	--[1]	8	--[1]	166	2.56	204	0.35	0	0
164N/107E L.9	3.0	5.34	26	0.02	19	0.03	195	2.89	92	0.14	3	--[1]

[1] Less than 0.01 g

by total weight of plant remains per sample, rather than by sample volume. To facilitate comparison with Scarry's data, both the sample volumes and total weight of plant remains per sample for the White site samples are listed in table 4.15.) Following Scarry (1986), I use medians rather than means to compare the two sites, since medians are less affected by extreme outlying values. Both the median and mean values for maize and nut remains from White and Moundville are listed in table 4.16, and the medians are compared in figure 4.7. The vertical scale in this figure is the natural logarithm of the quantity one plus the median count per liter (i.e., $\ln[1 + \text{median count per liter}]$). The log transformation is used because of the large differences between the values from the two sites, and one is added to the site medians before taking the logarithm in order to avoid negative logarithms.

It is clear from figure 4.7a that maize remains, hickory shell, and acorn shell are far more abundant at White than at Moundville. Acorn nutmeats are also more abundant at White than at Moundville, though the difference is not so great as for the other plant food remains. In part, the greater nut abundance at White is attributable to the nature of the excavated deposits. As an intentional refuse deposit, the White site refuse would be expected to have higher item counts per liter than the unintentional accumulations of sheet midden and pit fills from which most of the Moundville samples come. The accuracy of this expectation can be seen in figure 4.7b, in which the White site refuse data are compared to Moundville sheet midden data. Even floor deposits from the two sites are not strictly comparable. The floors sampled at Moundville were carefully laid deposits of clean sand, which were frequently renewed (Scarry 1986), while the White site floor deposits have more the character of gradual, unintentional accumulations. As figure 4.7c shows, the density of plant food remains in the Moundville floors is much lower.

Table 4.16 Mean and Median Counts per Liter for Maize and Nut Remains from White and Moundville Flotation Samples[1]

Context	Mean count per liter	Standard deviation	Median count per liter
Maize kernels			
White (Moundville III)[2]			
Refuse	5.5	2.6	6.5
Floors	4.3	2.9	3.4
All samples	4.8	2.6	3.7
Moundville (Moundville I)[3]			
Midden	1.5	2.1	1.0
Floors	1.3	2.8	0.3
All samples	1.4	2.2	0.6
Maize cupules			
White (Moundville III)			
Refuse	16.3	11.3	17.8
Floors	5.2	2.4	5.2
All samples	9.9	9.0	6.3
Moundville (Moundville I)			
Midden	2.2	6.6	0.6
Floors	1.1	1.6	0.6
All samples	1.3	3.5	0.8
Hickory shell			
White (Moundville III)			
Refuse	19.0	9.8	16.5
Floors	59.6	32.9	58.1
All samples	42.2	32.3	29.8
Moundville (Moundville I)			
Midden	0.4	0.3	0.3
Floors	0.4	0.4	0.3
All samples	0.6	0.9	0.3
Acorn shell			
White (Moundville III)			
Refuse	26.2	29.2	19.3
Floors	67.8	27.6	73.7
All samples	50.0	34.0	58.3
Moundville (Moundville I)			
Midden	0.6	0.5	0.4
Floors	1.3	3.9	0.3
All samples	1.7	4.2	0.6

Context	Mean count per liter	Standard deviation	Median count per liter
Acorn meat			
White (Moundville III)			
Refuse	6.6	5.6	9.7
Floors	0.3	0.5	0.5
All samples	3.0	4.7	0.2
Moundville (I)			
Midden	<0.1	0.3	0
Floors	0	0	0
All samples	<0.1	0.1	0

[1] Moundville data from Scarry 1986
[2] Number of samples: refuse 3; floors 4; all samples 7
[3] Number of samples: midden 26; floors 28; all samples 103

While the absolute values of the medians are not strictly comparable between sites, the ratios of plant food remains should be. To compare the two sites in terms of the relative importance of nuts and maize, Scarry (personal communication, 1986) suggests using the ratios of counts of acorn shell, hickory shell, and maize cupules. These data are presented as Tukey box plots in figure 4.8. Tukey box plots are a convenient way of presenting information about data distributions (see Cleveland and McGill 1985, 832 and references therein). The median of each distribution is plotted as a " + " enclosed in parentheses, which show a 95-percent confidence interval for the median. The left and right sides of the open rectangle are, respectively, the 25th and 75th percentiles. The distance between these percentiles is called the midspread. Data points that are more than 1.5 times the midspread below the 25th percentile, or 1.5 times the midspread above the 75th percentile, are called outliers and are plotted as asterisks. The single horizontal lines extend from the central box to the farthest data points that are not outliers. The box plots in figure 4.8 show that the acorn shell:hickory shell ratios at the two

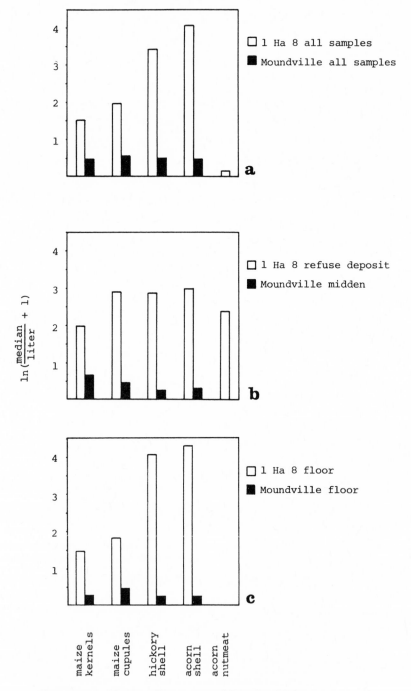

Figure 4.7 Median Counts per Liter for Maize and Nut Remains from White and Moundville Flotation Samples

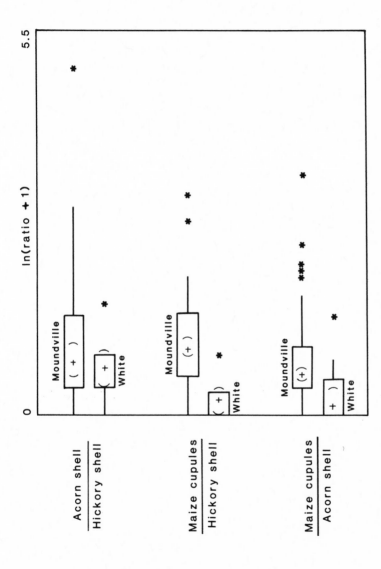

Figure 4.8 Box Plot of Acorn:Hickory Shell Ratios for White and Moundville Flotation Samples

sites are roughly equal, but that at Moundville both kinds of nutshells are scarce relative to maize cupules. This suggests that nuts as a class were more important in the diet at White than at Moundville.

It is tempting to see the apparently greater reliance on nuts at White as resulting from the previously discussed problem of frequent flooding of the site's catchment. While this is one potential explanation of the data, there are at least three other possibilities:

1. While the samples from Moundville are thought to include materials deposited during all parts of the year (Scarry 1986), the White site faunal data do not rule out the possibility that the site was occupied only seasonally. Thus the differing abundances of plant remains may be due to differing seasonality of occupation.

2. The contexts sampled at Moundville are nearly all at the north end of the site, in locations that were not residential precincts for commoners (Scarry 1986). The White site refuse, in contrast, is thought to include refuse from commoner as well as elite households. Therefore, the differing plant data may result from status-related differences in dietary rules, preferences, or prerogatives.

3. The Moundville samples date to the Moundville I phase, while the White samples are from late Moundville III. Therefore, the differences may simply result from chronological change in the subsistence strategy. Caddell's (1983) data from the Lubbub site are relevant here. Unfortunately, differences between Scarry's processing methods and those of Caddell probably introduce biases that preclude direct comparison of their data. (Caddell identified remains retained on a 2-mm screen, while Scarry identified material retained on a 1.4-mm screen. Differences in the fragility and ease of identification of small pieces of nutshell compared with maize likely render Scarry's and Caddell's data noncomparable.) Caddell's (1983) data are relevant because she showed that Pro-

4. Corn, a symbolically important food, was given to the elites residing at Moundville in greater frequency than nuts (regional, rather than intra-site, perspective),

Subsistence 131

tohistoric (Summerville IV phase) samples had slightly higher nut:maize ratios than the earlier Summerville II/III samples. The White site data come from around the time this change was occurring at Lubbub. The differences between Caddell's and Scarry's analytic procedures make it difficult to determine, but the increased nut utilization in the Protohistoric at Lubbub does not appear to be as substantial as the difference between the late Moundville III White samples and the Moundville I samples from Moundville. Despite the apparent parallel between the Lubbub and White/Moundville data, a region-wide shift in subsistence strategy should be regarded as a possibility not yet securely demonstrated.

The last detail of the botanical analysis to be discussed is the representation of maize varieties at the White site. Using four morphological variables (row number, cupule height, cupule width, maximum cob diameter), Scarry (1986) performed a k-means cluster analysis on all available, measurable Moundville-era and Protohistoric cobs from the Black Warrior River valley. The four-cluster solution showed the clearest patterning by sample context and cluster definition. One cluster is distinguished by high row number (average = 12.5) and appears to represent a distinct variety of maize. It is present throughout the Moundville era and is found at White as well as at Moundville. (The measurable cobs from White came from two smudge pits, one radiocarbon dated to the Moundville II phase and the other of undetermined age.) The other three clusters appear to represent chronological stages in the evolution of Eastern Complex maize, with one cluster comprising primarily Moundville I samples, another comprising primarily known or probable Moundville II and III samples, and the final cluster comprising mostly Protohistoric samples. Most of the "Moundville II/III cluster" come from White. On this basis, it can be concluded that both of the varieties of maize consumed at Moundville were also consumed at White.

Conclusion

The goal of this chapter was to determine whether there were patterned differences between sites of the Moundville chiefdom either in potentially available subsistence resources or in the foods actually consumed. Catchment analyses indicate that the single-mound sites of the Moundville chiefdom were in very similar locations. All would have had direct access to the same set of wild food resources, and the positive correlation between intrinsic fertility of the catchments and size of the occupations is consistent with these sites being agriculturally self-sufficient. One site, 1Tu42/43, seems to be an exception to the fertility-occupation size correlation, but the estimated size of the site is likely to be erroneous. The White site has a catchment significantly more flood-prone than the others, which may have made maize cultivation there less dependable. Maize remains were in fact less abundant relative to nutshell at this site, compared to the botanical remains from Scarry's excavations north of Mound R at Moundville. Scarry's data, however, are from an earlier time, probably from households of a different social status, and possibly not from the same season(s). Thus it is not clear whether the relative abundance of nutshell at White results from reliance on nuts to buffer shortfalls in maize production, or whether other factors are involved. In summary, the botanical and catchment data provide no reason to suspect that any of the single-mound sites appreciably depended on nonlocal plant foods.

Occupants of the single-mound sites would have had direct access to the same faunal resources. Faunal remains from White are similar in overall composition to those from other Mississippian sites in west Alabama. That is, all the communities from which data are available seem to have consumed nearly identical proportions of fish, fowl, deer, small mammals, etc. There are, however, marked differences between sites in terms of the portions of deer that are consumed. A farmstead (Yarborough) and a single-mound site (Lubbub) along the Tombigbee River had complementary patterns of enrichment (single-mound site) and depletion (farmstead) of the meatiest parts of a deer carcass. This pattern is interpreted as evidence of provisioning of the elite at the single-mound site. The upper forelimb in particular seems to have been preferentially consumed by the elite. Unfortunately, White is the only site in the Moundville chiefdom from which an adequate faunal sample is available. The White site deer remains have a greater-than-expected proportion of upper hind limb elements, but a lower-than-expected proportion of upper forelimb. Several possibilities may account for this pattern, among them:

1. In contrast to the central Tombigbee River valley, in the Moundville chiefdom the upper *hind* limb may have been the portion preferentially consumed by the elite.

2. Upper forelimbs may have been preferentially consumed by the elite at White, but the bones were not discarded in the refuse deposit sampled in 1983.

3. As the most preferred portion of the deer, upper forelimbs may have been sent to the higher-ranking elite at Moundville.

Until adequate faunal samples from Moundville and from farmsteads or hamlets are available, it is difficult to determine what accounts for the patterning in the White site faunal data. Tentatively, however, it appears that deer meat was being moved between sites of the chiefdom. The movement does not appear to be bulk redistribution to the populace at large, but rather the provisioning of elite persons with preferred cuts of meat.

5 Craft Production

Introduction

The production of nonsubsistence goods is examined in this chapter. Rather than repeating the cumbersome term *nonsubsistence goods,* I will use the term *craft items.* In common usage, this term carries connotations about the mode of production and visual attractiveness of the items, so that we think of a craft item as something produced by an individual artisan and which a tourist or a museum might like to buy. Such connotations are *not* implied in my use of the term. This point is important, since connotations about the mode of production would prejudge the issue being examined.

As with subsistence goods, the several models of chiefdom economies specify different patterns of craft production. The redistribution model specifies that the districts composing a chiefdom differ in their production of utilitarian crafts, i.e., cooking utensils, clothing, and agricultural and hunting implements. The mobilization model specifies that each district is self-sufficient in these goods. The tributary model places much of the production of prestige goods in settlements other than the paramont center. The prestige goods model puts such production either at the paramount center or outside the chiefdom. These predictions are compared below with data from the Moundville chiefdom.

Before proceeding to the analysis, however, it is necessary to describe the severity of the problem posed by the nonpreservation of organic materials. Aside from a few objects preserved by waterlogging and charring or by copper salts in burials at Moundville, there are no preserved fabric, leather, cordage, cane or wooden objects, or basketry, and bone tools are probably underrepresented due to poor preservation. These are major deficiencies in the data, since they include all clothing and most of the tools used to make it, most of the agricultural, fishing, and hunting gear, and the wooden mortars in which maize was pounded for the daily meals (cf. Swanton 1946, 439–608). Such deficiencies in the data base are, of course, common in the archaeological record, and several procedures have been devised to bridge the resulting gaps. Catchment analysis, for instance, can reveal whether raw materials for the nonpreserved items were locally available. Another approach is to examine the production of nondurable items by studying the durable tools used in their fabrication. Such tools and other durable crafts are examined here, after a brief consideration of site catchments.

As the previous chapter shows, the settlements composing the Moundville chiefdom had catchments with similar biotic resources. Faunal and botanical materials used for clothing (e.g., deer hides, mulberry bark), hide-working tools (e.g., deer metapodial scrapers, bone needles), cordage (e.g., deer sinew, squirrel hide), mats and baskets (e.g., rushes, cane), and household utensils (e.g., wooden dishes, cane knives, wooden mortars and pestles) would have been equally available to all the settlements. Furthermore, the sites do not differ in the accessibility of the raw materials for durable craft items such as pottery and stone tools. Clays suitable for pottery, and which apparently were used for pottery at Moundville (Steponaitis 1983a, 18–20), crop out from Tuscaloosa at the north to just south of the White site (Clarke 1966, 1970). The predominant material used for chipped stone tools is pebble chert and quartzite from

the Tuscaloosa sand and gravel formation. This formation blankets the Fall Line Hills from above Tuscaloosa
to below the White site, and derived gravels can also be
found in streambeds leading from the hills and in
Pleistocene alluvium in the river floodplain itself. The
two other lithic materials used for domestic implements
are greenstone (for axes) and a brown siltstone from
which hoes that may date to the Moundville period were
sometimes made. The siltstone is actually just floodplain silts cemented with iron and manganese oxides
and can be found all along the banks of the Black Warrior River. Greenstone—more precisely, chlorite schist
and other closely related fine-grained metamorphics—
crops out in eastern Alabama (Jones 1939). Since the
nearest outcrop is over 100 km east of Moundville, all
the Moundville communities were essentially equally
distant from the stone source. There is, therefore, no obvious geographic disparity in animal, vegetal, or mineral resources that might encourage communities to
specialize in different crafts.

Ethnographically, however, community craft specialization often has little obvious relation to the distribution of raw materials. Thus, to be confident that
communities or districts of the Moundville chiefdom did
not have different craft specializations, we must rely on
the archaeological record of craft production. Data from
the subsidiary sites come from excavations at White and
systematic surface collections from the other single-
mound sites. From Moundville itself, there are two
classes of information: artifacts from excavations directed by Margaret Scarry in 1978–79; and information
gleaned by Christopher Peebles from the records of excavations prior to 1951. Since these pre-1951 excavations
did not involve screening of excavated deposits, the information from them is not quantitatively comparable to
the more recent screened excavations. The extensive
early excavations, however, remain an important source

of qualitative information about craft items at Moundville.

Ceramics

Since potsherds are the most abundant artifacts at archaeological sites of the Moundville chiefdom, ceramic
production is the first craft to be analyzed. Steponaitis
(1983a, 33) studied technological and functional aspects
of Moundville pottery and described the ceramics as follows:

> Moundville pottery can be divided into two broad groups,
> which differ from each other in both function and paste
> composition. One group consists mostly of bowls and
> bottles that were used as eating and storage vessels, but
> were not used for cooking. Typically, these noncooking
> vessels are tempered with finely ground shell, and have a
> dark surface finish produced by deliberate smudging
> and reduction during firing. Indeed, the fact that most of
> them are "black-filmed" implies that they were not used
> for cooking, because contact with a cooking fire would
> have oxidized the surface and made it lighter.
> The second group, the cooking ware, consists of un-
> burnished jars. These vessels, in contrast to the non-
> cooking wares, are usually tempered with coarse shell,
> and tend to have an oxidized, reddish brown surface
> color consistent with what one would expect on a vessel
> used over a fire.

Steponaitis (1983a, 33–45) showed that the mechanical properties of these two wares were consistent with
his functional designations: initially, the cooking ware
is not as resistant to mechanical shock as the serving/
storage ware, but it does not deteriorate as quickly when
exposed to rapid heating and cooling (thermal shock),
such as a cooking vessel undergoes.

One of the goals of Peebles's (1978c, 4) Moundville research program was to determine whether pottery was produced by craft specialists, and what role chiefly control of its production may have had:

> It has been proposed (Peebles and Kus 1977) that one of the major areas of craft specialization in chiefdoms was the manufacture of ceramics. If either part or all of the pottery production at Moundville was in the hands of such specialists, then the limited number of artisans should be reflected in the stylistic, morphological, and technical variability of the pottery. In addition, if part or all of the pottery production was removed from the context of the individual household, then the kilns and other remnants of the manufacture of ceramics should be localized within the site. Finally, if the complex social organization known to exist at Moundville developed there through time, and if specialized production of ceramics is associated with such development, then there should be a reduction in the variability of ceramics and a trend to the localization of pottery production within the site through time.

While these propositions cannot yet be tested definitively, there is evidence bearing on each. First, both technological and stylistic evidence indicates that part-time craft specialists were indeed making some of the Moundville pottery. The technological evidence consists of van der Leeuw's (1979, 1981) and Hardin's (1979, 1981) identification of a highly efficient, skillful technique for fabricating fine-ware vessels. Beginning with vessel fabrication by adding coils to a basal slab supported on a rest, the technique progressed by increasing the fraction of the vessel formed on the rest. By the late Moundville II and Moundville III phases, some vessels were being made in molds. A subglobular bottle, for instance, would be made by forming the lower half of the vessel body in a hemispherical mold, forming the upper half in the same or a similar mold, cutting out from the upper half a hole for the insertion of the bottle neck, attaching the upper and lower hemispheres, and attaching a slab-built cylindrical neck. In contrast, cooking vessels were made by coiling with paddle-and-anvil finishing. In comparing the two techniques, van der Leeuw (1981, 107) says of the mold technique: "It seems as if this technique in particular was in the hands of specialists. There was a considerably higher degree of skill involved, and a much greater volume of information processing was required, especially when decoration was added to the vessels."

Stylistic evidence of ceramic craft specialists is provided by Hardin's (1979, 1981) analysis of decorated fineware vessels. Assisted by Steponaitis, Hardin identified sets of vessels decorated by individual artisans, by looking for (nearly) identical attributes of motif selection, choice of structural options in rendering the motif, and technique in executing the motif. Because all three variables must be considered, individual "hands" cannot be identified reliably across different vessel shapes or across different varieties in the Moundville type-variety typology (varieties by definition have different motifs). Hardin identified twelve sets of vessels and, less certainly, an additional four sets, where each set was decorated by a single individual (table 5.1). Six sets were identified for Moundville Engraved *var. Hemphill,* one set definitely and three less certainly for *var. Taylorville,* one set for *var. Wiggins,* two definitely and one less certainly for *var. Tuscaloosa,* one set for *var. Northport,* and one set for Carthage Incised *var. Carthage.* While these sets were identified solely on stylistic grounds, "independent corroboration of the stylistic identification of sets by the same hand was provided by similarities of vessel form, surface texture (probably reflecting clay, surface treatment, and firing conditions), and building technique used for the vessel bodies" (Hardin 1981, 110).

Table 5.1 Sets of Vessels from Moundville Decorated by Individual Potters[1]

Type variety	No. of vessels in sample	No. of unmatched vessels (% of total)	Catalog numbers of vessels by set (each row is one set)
Moundville Engraved *Hemphill*	138	124 (89.9)	SD1/M7; SD6/M7 NR30/M5; SD34/M7; WR81 SWM15A/M7; SD58/M7 O9/M5; SD71/M7; WR8/M7 RW878; NN'18 SD44/M7; SD87/M7
Moundville Engraved *Wiggins*	47	38 (80.9)	(all one set) Rho102; Rho304; SED6; SED34; SD96/M7; EE9; EE86; EE136; SWM220

Moundville Engraved *Taylorville*	28	15 (53.6)	Rho66; SD10/M5; NE8; EE429; EI15; SWM183 (probable set) WR9; NE133; EE133 (probable set) WR60; SE3 (probable set) Rho364; Snow6
Moundville Engraved *Tuscaloosa*	21	15 (71.4)	NE572; SE13 Rho440; SL25 (probable set) O14/M5; SD841
Moundville Engraved *Northport*	16	13 (81.3)	C17/M5; <M>17/3348; WP119
Carthage Incised *Carthage*	19	17 (89.5)	WP83; WP85

[1] M. Hardin, personal communication; V. Steponaitis, personal communication

Table 5.2 Data for Testing the Likelihood of Nonspecialized Production of Vessels of Six Varieties at Moundville

Type variety	No. of vessels in collection	No. of identified potters
Moundville Engraved *Hemphill*	138	130
Moundville Engraved *Wiggins*	47	39
Moundville Engraved *Taylorville*	28	19
Moundville Engraved *Tuscaloosa*	21	18
Moundville Engraved *Northport*	16	14
Carthage Incised *Carthage*	19	18

[1] Test for difference of proportions, normal distribution
[2] Binomial test

Since the patterns of fabrication and of decoration appear to be wholly redundant, I refer to these sets of vessels as being produced by a single potter. This is merely for convenience, since the data do not indicate how many people were involved in the production of each set, but only that each set came from the same workshop.

To gain an idea of the quantitative contribution of these individual potters (or fabrication-decoration workshops), we can compare the number of vessels decorated by individual hands with the number of vessels from which the sets were identified. This information is presented in table 5.2. A measure of the statistical significance of these quantities, given the sample sizes, is possible using the null hypothesis that each one of K potters produced 1/K of all pots. Under this hypothesis, we would expect only 1/K of the pots in a random sample to have been made by a single potter. Since we do not know how many potters there actually were at Moundville, we can conservatively estimate K by the number of potters observed in the sample, or k. The actual number of potters was certainly higher than this estimate, and the higher the value of K, the less likely it

Expected % of pots per potter	Largest no. of pots by one potter	% of total pots by one potter	Significance level
0.77	3	2.17	.029[1]
2.56	9	19.15	.002[1]
5.26	6	21.43	.003[2]
5.56	2	9.52	.219[2]
7.14	3	18.75	.078[2]
5.56	2	10.53	.200[2]

would be to find a large set of pots made by a single potter. Thus, if we can reject the null hypothesis using $K = k$, we can be even more confident that the null hypothesis would be rejected if we knew the true value of K. For each of the varieties, we can use binomial theory to determine the likelihood of obtaining the largest single set, given the sample size and given the null hypothesis estimate that $1/k$ of the pots in the sample were produced by a single potter. (Actually, for Moundville Engraved *var. Hemphill* and *var. Wiggins,* the sample sizes are large enough that it is appropriate to use a test for difference of proportions using the normal distribution.) Results of the tests are presented in table 5.2. For three of the varieties we can reject the null hypothesis at the .05 level.

These test results suggest that some potters made more pots than others. In interpreting these results, one should recall that for three of the five varieties there is more than one identified set, and that the tests only determine the probability of obtaining the largest set. Furthermore, the extreme conservativeness of the assumption that $K = k$ should be pointed out. Peebles and Kus (1977, 435) estimated the population of Moundville during the period when these pots were made as over 1,000.

If each household consisted of five individuals and each household produced its own pots (i.e., no craft specialization), then at any one time there would have been at least 200 potters. The pots were produced over a period of at least 200 years, or roughly ten generations of 200 potters per generation. Compared to these estimates, the estimates of K used in the tests are extremely conservative, and hence the actual probability of observing such large sets of pots from a single potter should be far lower than the values in table 5.2.

On these grounds, we can conclude that, unless cultural or natural factors have strongly biased our recovery of whole pots, a limited number of potters produced a disproportionately large number of fine-ware vessels. The latter case, of course, would effectively indicate craft specialization of some degree. I can think of no natural factors that would result in the overrepresentation of the pots of only a few pottery workshops. Nearly all of the recovered vessels are from burials, so different contexts of deposition would not account for the observed abundances. Two cultural factors might be of importance, however. The disproportionate representation of a few potters' products in burials might not be due to differential productivity between potters, but due to strong biases in which potters' vessels were selected for inclusion in graves. The best way to assess this possibility would be to compare the pottery from domestic refuse deposits with that from the burials, a task made difficult by the near absence of whole vessels from refuse contexts. Short of this, it should be noted that the vessels in graves are not mortuary vessels per se. Extensive abrasion and chipping on the base and lip indicate that many of these vessels received protracted use before being interred, just as midden sherds of the same vessel types reveal traces of use. If there were a systematic selection of certain potters' pots for inclusion with burials, would we expect these pots to have undergone the same use-history as other potters' pots? Rather than attempting to answer this question, it seems safer to allow the issue of differential production versus differential selection for burial to remain unresolved until a direct comparison of burial and domestic-refuse pots can be made.

The other cultural factor that might account for the observed abundances of vessels produced by a few individuals is that often more than one pot was found per grave. If all or most of the vessels from each identified set had come from a single grave, then there would be little basis for inferring specialist potters. The gravelots might simply contain domestically produced pottery. This is not the case, however; no two vessels of any one set came from the same grave, nor is there even much spatial clustering of the pots in the sets. Pots of a set are as likely to be found on opposite sides of the site as they are to be on the same side. Moreover, two vessels of one set of Moundville Engraved *var. Taylorville* were found at different sites, one at Moundville and the other at 1Tu2 (Snows Bend), a single-mound site 20 km north of Moundville. Except for the unresolved issue raised in the previous paragraph, no identifiable factor other than some form of craft specialization accounts for the observed data.

As noted above, Peebles (1978c, 4) inferred that specialization in pottery production ought to result in kilns or other remnants of the manufacture of ceramics being localized within the site. While no unambiguous kilns have been found at Moundville, there is a set of six large, irregularly shaped, fired areas in a small zone west of Mound P (see figure 5.1; Peebles 1979, 817−25). Most of these were outside of any walled structure, and those apparently within walls may be superpositions. Only three of the areas were associated with prepared basin-shaped hearths, which is the standard form of hearth at the site. The fired areas are not just incidental burning around domestic hearths, however, since one of the

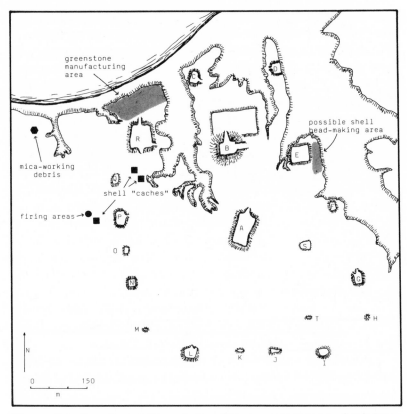

Figure 5.1   Location at Moundville of Features Related to Craft Pro-
                 duction

areas associated with a hearth was 5.7 x 1.2 m and the
firing extended 15 to 25 cm deep. No such large fired
areas have been described elsewhere at the site, with the
possible exception of "flat fire places, one at least having
clay hardened like brick from continued heat" north of
Mound R (Moore 1905, 221). While Moore distinguished
these "fire places" from the basin-shaped hearths typical
at the site, no information about their size was provided.
The fact that the only strong candidates for pottery firing areas at Moundville were located within a few dozen

meters of each other is particularly striking, considering that roughly 5 ha of the site has been excavated.

One other line of evidence about the localization of pottery production within the Moundville site is the distribution of "caches" of clay and mussel shell. These are the raw materials for pottery. Aside from "two bags" of a clay and crushed-shell mixture recovered east of Mound E (Peebles 1979, 298), all clay and shell caches were found west of the plaza (see figure 5.1). Most of these were within 100 m of the firing areas, though another set was some 200 m to the northeast (south of Mound R). While the clay-shell mixture from east of Mound E is almost certainly raw material for pottery, caches of clay or shell alone are not necessarily related to ceramic production. Clay is also used as daub for structure walls, and mussel shell is a food by-product. In light of the uncertain relation of these caches to pottery production, and their rather diffuse association with the firing areas, I regard this line of evidence as weak support for the presence of pottery specialists at the site.

In contrast to the case for Moundville, there is little available information about the presence and organization of ceramic production at the outlying sites. Some pots were made in at least one of the single-mound sites, because the 1932 AMNH burial excavations at the Snows Bend site (1Tu2/3) encountered a "nice bowl in kiln" (original field notes, quoted in DeJarnette and Peebles [1970, 107]). The bowl was held fast in an area of fired clay, about which no further details were recorded. Since the excavators were already familiar with the standard Moundville basin-shaped hearth, their use of the term *kiln* suggests this feature was not a hearth. There is every reason to believe that the excavators' functional interpretation was correct (though *firing area* might be a more apt term than *kiln*). A burial at this site also contained one vessel of a pair identified by Hardin (1981) as decorated by the same artisan; the other vessel of the pair was found at Moundville. On these grounds, we can conclude that some pots were made in at least one of the single-mound sites, and that some potters or finished pots moved between this site and Moundville.

However, information on the extent of pottery production at Snows Bend and the other single-mound sites is not available. While identification of the products of individual potters can in principle be done with sherds (Hardin 1979), such analysis is not feasible with the available samples. The surface collections from single-mound sites are so extensively fragmented as to preclude useful results. The excavated sample from the White site is of such late date that the fine-line incised (so-called engraved) designs principally used by Hardin are no longer part of the decorative repertoire. Similarly, the use of molds for vessel forming, which appears to figure in the development of specialization of pottery making at Moundville, is most easily detected on whole vessels, particularly on subglobular bottles. Subglobular bottles were no longer being made during the time the White site midden and refuse deposits were formed (see chapter three; Steponaitis 1983a, figure 26). Some of the hemispherical bowls and short-neck bowls at the White site may have been mold-made: shoulders of short-neck bowls are often broken evenly at the point of vertical tangency where shoulder meets lower body, a fracture pattern common among mold-made jars. This pattern is not diagnostic of the use of molds, however; the point of vertical tangency on short-neck bowls is often rather angular and is thus mechanically weaker, hence more prone to breakage, than the smoothly curved upper and lower body walls. Fracture at this inflection point would be common irrespective of the technique of vessel construction.

To summarize, ceramic samples from the outlying sites are either too fragmentary or of the wrong period to determine how they relate to the specialization of pottery production at Moundville, and the extent of excavation at the outlying sites is not sufficient to reveal the extent and organization of pottery production there. At Moundville itself, the abundance of vessels produced by a small number of individuals indicates that there were a limited number of potters during late Moundville II and Moundville III times. The use of a highly efficient vessel-forming technique for certain classes of vessels during this period is consistent with the rapid production of a large number of these vessels by a few individuals. Extensive excavation at the Moundville site has revealed what appear to be pottery firing areas in only one very small portion of this large and populous site. This strongly supports the conclusion that, during late Moundville II and III times, a disproportionate fraction of the community's pots were produced by a small number of individuals. Finally, to prevent confusion on this issue (cf. Muller 1984, 1986; Yerkes 1986), I emphasize that I make no claim as to whether these potters were full-time specialists or only part-time specialists; I merely argue that there was some specialization of pottery production.

Stone Tools

Stone tools are highly durable in the archaeological record, and their production and distribution are thus important lines of evidence about the organization of the Moundville economy. This evidence, however, has a number of limitations that require discussion before we can proceed to drawing positive conclusions. In chapter three, it was mentioned that surface collections from subsidiary sites of the Moundville chiefdom had lithic assemblages containing high proportions of material from other time periods. To gain an idea of how high these proportions are, the ratio of Moundville-era sherds to the total number of sherds can be used as an index of mixing. The surface collections from occupation areas at single-mound sites have between 4 and 67 percent Moundville-era sherds (Bozeman 1982). Even if the mixture of lithic artifacts were no worse than these figures, it would be difficult to extract useful information from these assemblages.

However, there is reason to suspect that the actual percentage of stone artifacts dating to the Moundville period may be much lower than the sherd ratios. In most cases, the principal non-Moundville-era ceramics at these sites are of Late Woodland age (West Jefferson phase—A.D. 850 or 900 to 1050). In surface collections at 1Je31, 1Je32, and 1Je33 (the type sites of the West Jefferson phase), the lithic:ceramic ratios are 1.71:1, 7.67:1, and 10.17:1, respectively (Jenkins and Nielsen 1974). In the excavation contexts at White that have nearly pure West Jefferson ceramic assemblages, there are three to five times as many stone items as sherds. In contrast, more-or-less pure Moundville-era deposits have lithic:ceramic ratios that are the inverse of these figures. Surface collections from small, sparse sherd scatters interpreted as Moundville-era farmsteads have roughly one-third as many stone items as sherds. In the least-mixed Moundville-era deposits at White, there are from one-third to one-fifth as many stone artifacts as sherds. In excavations north of Mound R at Moundville, the lithic:ceramic ratio was 1:0.03 (Scarry 1986). If we assume that these ratios are representative of other West Jefferson and Moundville components on the Black Warrior River floodplain, then a simple calculation indicates that none of the surface collections should have lithic assemblages that contain more than 28 percent Moundville-era stone artifacts.

Actually, the situation is much more complicated than the blithe comparison above indicates. Some of these ratios come from surface collections, while others represent remains retained on screens. These two kinds of data are not comparable. There are also problems in comparing some of the screened samples to other screened samples. The deposits north of Mound R at Moundville are structure floors and incidental midden layers, while the Moundville-era deposits at White are intentional refuse deposits. The different formation processes may bias the lithic:sherd ratios, though which way and how severely is not known. Notwithstanding these complications, the consistent difference between the West Jefferson phase and the Moundville-era data and the fact that this difference spans several orders of magnitude are here taken as evidence that most of the lithic artifacts in the surface collections from Moundville's subsidiary sites come from other components.

Ordinarily, formal (i.e., carefully retouched) tools can be expected to differ in shape between periods. In such an instance, the mixed nature of the surface collections would make it difficult to extract any information about Moundville-era debitage and informal tools, but we could still obtain information about formal tools from the Moundville components. Unfortunately, the principal formal tool type—a small triangular projectile point—was used throughout west Alabama in both the Moundville period and the preceding Late Woodland period. Comparisons of points from known-age contexts have not identified patterned morphological or technological differences between periods (Ensor 1981; Allan 1983).

Other formal stone tools are present in the collections, including drills, gravers, celts, and hoes. Researchers in west Alabama have some knowledge about the temporal distributions of these tools, but this is far from complete. Ground and polished greenstone celts definitely were used during both the Moundville period and the preceding Late Woodland, since they are present in well-dated excavation contexts (Jenkins and Nielsen 1974; Jenkins and Ensor 1981; Moore 1905, 1907; DeJarnette and Peebles 1970; Scarry 1986; unpublished field notes on file at Mound State Monument). Two forms of drills may date to the Moundville period: reworked projectile points and cylindrical drills. None of the cylindrical drills have been found in clear Moundville contexts, and distributional studies by Pope (1989) suggest that they are of Late Woodland (West Jefferson phase) date. A few drills made from resharpened projectile points, as well as a few gravers or piercing implements, were recovered from the late Moundville III trash deposit at the White site, though most such tools at the site came from mixed midden primarily of Late Woodland origin. It would be premature to conclude that such tools definitely were used during the Moundville period. Another class of stone tool found at Moundville-era sites is a large silt-stone implement thought to be a hoe blade (M. Pope, personal communication). While their presence in excavations at Moundville indicates that at least some of these tools were in use at that time, it is not known whether they were also in use earlier.

So far this discussion has emphasized the difficulties of extracting useful information from the stone tool assemblages. Despite these difficulties, it is possible to draw a fairly clear picture of the use of stone artifacts in the Moundville period. The rest of this discussion focuses on the evidence that leads to the following conclusions:

1. Most cutting tools were not made of stone.

2. Most tools made of chipped stone were made of locally available materials.

3. Tools made of nonlocal stone (either ground or chipped) were made primarily at Moundville.

Two lines of evidence show that most cutting tools ① were not made of stone. First, as has been stated above, stone tools and debitage are infrequent at sites of the ⓐ Moundville period, in comparison with earlier sites (using lithic counts standardized by sherd counts). This appears to hold true regardless of the level of a site in the Moundville settlement hierarchy. A second line of evidence that stone tools were not the most common cutting tools in the Moundville era consists of ethnohistoric ⓑ descriptions of tool use in the southeastern United States. Swanton (1946, 564) summarized this evidence briefly: "Undoubtedly knives of shell, stone, and perhaps bone were employed, but cane or reed knives are the only aboriginal implements of this kind to be widely noted. They appear to have been in use everywhere throughout the [Southeast]." Swanton (1946, 571–84) also reviewed early European descriptions of arrowheads and lance points, among which cane tips were mentioned frequently.

The chipped stone tools that *were* used during the ② Moundville era were predominantly made of locally available raw material. Table 5.3 lists the raw material types of all retouched pieces from the late Moundville III refuse deposit at the White site. For 84 percent of these ⓐ items, the raw material is locally available. The predominance of local raw materials is also seen in the debitage, ⓑ of which 96.6 percent by count is chert or quartz from the Tuscaloosa gravels and only 3.4 percent is nonlocal material.

Problem

Conceivably, the admixture of earlier lithic material in the White site refuse deposit is "masking" a usage of nonlocal stone higher than the summary statistics for the debitage indicate. The problem of chronological admixture of the lithic artifacts in the refuse deposit at the White site, already familiar to the reader, is underscored by the fact that two out of the fourteen (14 percent) diagnostic projectile points are pre-Mississippian (i.e., the

Table 5.3   Raw Material Types for Chipped Stone from Late
Moundville III Refuse Deposit, White Site

Artifact type	Tuscaloosa gravel	Local stone Quartz	Camden
Tools			
Madison point	8	0	2
Flint River Spike	1	0	0
Projectile point/			
knife fragments	12	0	1
Drill/piercer	8	0	0
Chisel (?)	1	0	0
Graver	1	0	0
Preform/crude knife	6	1	1
Flake knife	1	0	0
All tools (%)	38 (74.5)	1 (2.0)	4 (7.8)
Debitage (%)	2,011 (89.4)	135 (6.0)	28 (1.2)

Late Woodland Flint River Spikes; Cambron and Hulse 1975, 53). While the refuse deposit data presented here all come from excavation units with 10 percent or less pre-Mississippian ceramics, some of these units are less mixed than others.

If the late Moundville III usage of nonlocal stone was proportionally greater than in earlier periods, there should be a *negative* correlation between the percentage of pre-Mississippian ceramics and the percentage of nonlocal debitage. Table 5.4 presents these percentage values for all those refuse deposit excavation units in which the number of sherds and the number of debitage pieces is each greater than thirty. This cutoff value is used to prevent the relatively high sampling error expectable for small samples from obscuring any real relationship. As can be seen by the least-squares regression line fitted to the data in figure 5.2, there appears to be a *positive* relationship between these variables. While the correlation is not significant ($r = .34$, $p = .14$), these

Ft. Payne	Bangor	Nonlocal stone Tallahatta quartzite	Coastal Plain white	Unidentified
0	1 (?)	0	0	1
0	0	0	1	0
1	1	1	0	0
1	0	0	0	0
0	0	0	0	0
0	0	0	0	0
0	0	0	0	0
1	0	0	0	0
3 (5.9)	2 (3.9)	1 (2.0)	1 (2.0)	1 (2.0)
4 (0.2)	6 (0.3)	21 (0.9)	14 (0.6)	31 (1.4)

data do indicate that admixture of earlier material more likely elevates the proportion of nonlocal debitage than reduces it. No more than a few percent of late Moundville III debitage was nonlocal material.

A technological analysis of the White site debitage indicates that all stages of the lithic reduction sequence for locally available raw material took place there. Table 5.5 presents the counts and weights of five debitage categories for the material above the floor level in squares 162N/105E and 164N/105E. These two units were selected because they are the least mixed of the excavation units in the refuse deposit. The shatter category includes both unmodified shatter from heating (nearly all the chert has been heat-treated) and unmodified debris from bipolar fracture of cobbles. The prevalence of bipolar core reduction probably accounts for the scarcity of prepared, flawed, or exhausted flake cores, only one of which is present. Shatter and decortication flakes together represent debris from the initial reduction of cob-

Table 5.4 Counts and Percentages of Nonlocal Debitage and Percentages of pre-Mississippian Sherds for Selected Units of the Late Moundville III Refuse Deposit, White Site

Analytical units	Local debitage (no.)	Nonlocal debitage (no.)	(%)	Pre-Mississippian sherds (%)
162N/105E L.1	109	2	1.8	2.3
L.2	248	9	3.5	2.3
L.3	72	2	2.7	3.2
164N/105E L.1	91	3	3.2	3.1
L.2	223	6	2.6	3.0
L.3	64	1	1.5	3.0
166N/105E L.1	85	2	2.3	4.1
L.2	181	8	4.2	5.0
L.3	195	5	2.5	4.3
162N/107E L.1	52	3	5.5	3.1
L.2	45	2	4.3	8.1
164N/107E L.1	28	1	3.4	4.9
L.2	32	0	0	1.7
166N/107E L.2	38	2	5.0	4.7
162N/107.5E L.1	106	5	4.5	6.0
L.2	73	2	2.7	2.0
164N/107.5E L.1	103	1	1.0	6.0
L.2	136	8	5.6	3.0
166N/107.5E L.2	148	9	5.7	5.0
L.3	36	0	0	2.5
Total	2,065	71	3.3	3.6

bles to "usable" flakes. Flakes of bifacial retouch (only flakes with intact high-angle platforms were included) represent the final stage in the manufacture of formal tools and also the resharpening of worn tools. Miscellaneous flakes as a group are intermediate in the lithic reduction sequence.

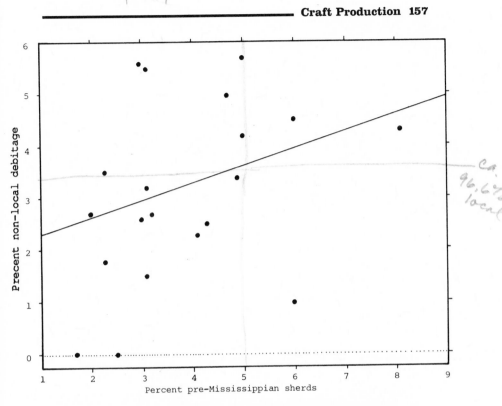

Figure 5.2 Scatterplot of Percentage of Nonlocal Debitage versus Percentage of pre-Mississippian Sherds for Selected Units of the Late Moundville III Refuse Deposit, White Site

For local raw material, the most abundant category of debitage, by count or weight, is shatter. Shatter and decortication flakes together compose two-thirds of the assemblage by count (84 percent by weight), and miscellaneous flakes make up most of the remainder. Thus the majority of the assemblage is debris from early and intermediate stages of biface manufacture. The final stage of tool production is represented by very little debris, though the criteria I employed for distinguishing bifacial retouch flakes probably underenumerate this class of data. These data, together with the presence of 348 unworked pebbles of local chert and quartz (mostly heat-treated but too small to be worked), indicate that all

Table 5.5 Counts and Weights of Local and Nonlocal Debitage from White Site, Levels 1–3 of 162N/105E and 164N/105E

Debitage category	Local stone				Nonlocal stone			
	no.	%[1]	wt.(g)	%[1]	no.	%[1]	wt.(g)	%[1]
Flake core	1	0.1	16.8	3.0	0	0	0	0
Shatter	351	43.5	372.5	67.1	1	4.2	0.5	5.0
Decortication	186	23.0	94.4	17.0	0	0	0	0
Miscellaneous flake	221	27.4	62.5	11.3	21	87.5	9.2	91.1
Flake of bifacial retouch	48	5.9	9.3	1.7	2	8.3	0.4	4.0
Total debitage	807	97.1	639.2	98.4	24	2.9	10.1	1.6

[1] Percentages calculated separately for local and nonlocal stone, except for totals

stages of the production of tools from local raw material took place at the White site.

The relative abundances of debitage categories for nonlocal material are distinctly different from those of local raw material (see table 5.5). Nearly all of the non-local debitage is from the intermediate or final stages of tool production. No unworked nonlocal material was found in these two excavation units. Keeping in mind that some of the nonlocal material is likely to be intrusive, the data indicate that very little nonlocal stone was worked at White, and what little there was had been brought to the site as prepared cores, blanks, or finished tools.

The data presented thus far support the conclusions that most cutting tools were not made of stone, and that, at least at the White site, most chipped stone tools were made of local raw material. Data from sites of the Moundville chiefdom also support a third conclusion, that nonlocal lithic raw material was made into finished items at Moundville but not at the outlying sites.

Excavations north of Mound R and south of the Conference Building at Moundville (Scarry 1986) yielded lithic assemblages that, though small, contrast sharply with the lithics from White. As can be seen in table 5.6, north of Mound R, nonlocal chert is three times as abundant as the local material, and south of the Conference Building, nonlocal material is only slightly less abundant than the local chert. Not only are these ratios markedly different from the local:nonlocal ratio at White, but much more of the nonlocal material in these excavations at Moundville is from the early stages of tool production than is the case at White. South of the Conference Building at Moundville, there was an exhausted flake core of nonlocal chert, something altogether absent from the White site assemblage. The abundance of nonlocal material in the debitage from Moundville is paralleled by the abundance of finished tools of nonlocal material.

Table 5.6 Counts and Weights of Local and Nonlocal Debitage from Excavations at Moundville[1]

Debitage category	Local stone				Nonlocal stone			
	no.	%[2]	wt.(g)	%[2]	no.	%[2]	wt.(g)	%[2]
North of Mound R								
Flake core	0	0	0	0	0	0	0	0
Shatter	6	24.0	3.9	13.6	20	26.3	40.5	50.6
Decortication	12	48.0	21.2	73.9	7	9.2	9.5	11.9
Miscellaneous	7	28.0	3.6	12.5	39	51.3	26.6	33.2
Flake of bifacial retouch	0	0	0	0	10	13.2	3.5	4.4
Total	25	24.8	28.7	26.4	76	75.2	80.1	73.6
South of the Conference Building								
Flake core	0	0	0	0	1	9.1	117.2	92.9
Shatter	0	0	0	0	0	0	0	0
Decortication	8	66.7	8.2	88.2	1	9.1	0.3	0.2
Miscellaneous flake	2	16.7	0.5	5.4	7	63.6	8.0	6.3
Flake of bifacial retouch	2	16.7	0.6	6.5	2	18.2	0.3	0.2
Total	12	52.2	9.3	6.9	11	47.8	126.2	93.1

1 From Scarry (1986)
2 Percentages calculated separately for local and nonlocal stone, except for totals

ca. 50-75%
non-local

We can examine the abundance at Moundville of chipped stone tools made of nonlocal material by looking at the artifacts from the Roadway excavation. A road was built at the Moundville site in the 1930s, and much of the roadbed was excavated prior to construction activities. Since the road loops around the site—sometimes inside the plaza, sometimes outside—the Roadway excavation constitutes a spatially extensive and in some sense representative sample of the site. The excavated deposits were not screened, and not surprisingly, there is virtually no debitage in the artifact collection. Among the chipped stone tools, there are fifty small triangular arrowheads, almost certainly of Moundville date. Of these, twenty-eight (56 percent) are made of locally available stone. The remainder are from north Alabama sources (Ft. Payne and Bangor: 26 percent [includes three arrowheads that may be Dover chert from Tennessee]) or are made of nonlocal material not yet identified (18 percent). The Roadway collection also contains seven exhausted cores, core fragments, and core-rejuvenation flakes. All seven are Ft. Payne chert from north Alabama. Clearly, at Moundville there is a far greater abundance of nonlocal chert than at White. It is also clear that at least some of this nonlocal chert was brought to the site as cores or unmodified cobbles rather than as blanks or finished tools.

In addition to the differences already described, the chipped stone assemblages from Moundville and the White site differ in terms of the relative abundances of particular nonlocal sources. Table 5.7 presents counts and percentages of chipped stone by source for the White site late Moundville III refuse deposit, the 1978–79 excavations in late Moundville I contexts north of Mound R at Moundville, and the 1978–79 excavations in Moundville I contexts south of the Conference Building at Moundville. At the White site, Ft. Payne and Bangor cherts are less abundant than Tallahatta quartzite and

Table 5.7 Counts and Percentages of Chipped Stone by Source, for White Site and Two Excavation Areas at Moundville

Site and phase		Tuscaloosa gravel	Local stone Quartz	Camden
White site	no.	2049	136	32
late Moundville III	%	89.1	5.9	1.4
Moundville NR[1]	no.	17	1	7
Moundville I	%	16.5	1.0	6.8
Moundville SCB[1]	no.	8	2	3
Moundville I	%	32.0	8.0	12.0

[1] From Scarry (1986); NR is North of Mound R, SCB is South of Conference Building

chert or agate from the Coastal Plain of south Alabama. In both Moundville collections, the Ft. Payne and Bangor material outnumbers the Coastal Plain and Tallahatta sources. Both Ft. Payne and Bangor cherts come from north Alabama, in the Tennessee River valley. Tallahatta quartzite, like the Coastal Plain material, comes from south Alabama. Thus the nonlocal chert at Moundville is predominantly from northern sources, while the nonlocal chipped stone at White is predominantly from sources to the south.

This does not necessarily mean that Moundville-era residents of the two sites tended to utilize different nonlocal materials. Nearly all of the Tallahatta quartzite projectile points recovered in surface collections in the Moundville area are Archaic stemmed forms, such as those of the Flint Creek, Little Bear Creek, Benton, and Morrow Mountain–White Springs clusters described by Ensor (1981, 94–100). I suspect that much of the Tallahatta quartzite, and by extension other south Alabama material, in the Moundville area dates before A.D. 1. How

| Ft. Payne | Bangor | Nonlocal stone | | Unidentified |
		Tallahatta quartzite	Coastal Plain white	
6	8	22	15	32
0.3	0.3	1.0	0.7	1.4
43	27	0	0	8
41.7	26.2	0	0	7.3
3	4	2	2	1
12.0	16.0	8.0	8.0	4.0

much of the predominance of south Alabama material at White is the result of admixture of earlier materials is not clear. White does lie to the south of Moundville, so it is certainly possible that Moundville-era residents at White might have had greater access to southern sources than the residents at Moundville. It is also possible that the procurement of nonlocal stone shifted during the Moundville period, for the samples from Moundville date to the Moundville I phase, while the White site material is of late Moundville III date. Analysis of lithic collections from other periods at Moundville and at other single-mound sites will be necessary to determine which of these factors is responsible for the observed differences between the White site nonlocal chipped stone and the samples from Moundville.

The 1978–79 excavations north of Mound R at Moundville also produced an unusual assemblage of ground and polished stone. Fully 25 percent (46/186) of all stone north of Mound R was greenstone or other metamorphic rock (Scarry 1986). In contrast, only 0.7 per-

cent of the lithics in the late Moundville III refuse
deposit at White were greenstone. The unusual abundance of greenstone north of Mound R at Moundville
was also noted by C. B. Moore, who found forty to fifty
celt fragments in his excavations there and described
this abundance as "new in our experience" (Moore 1905,
221). Table 5.8 presents further information about the
abundance of greenstone at Moundville and other sites
in the Black Warrior River valley. The excavations north
of Mound R at Moundville (roughly 6 m³) produced considerably more greenstone by weight as well as by count
than the 1983 excavations at the White site (roughly 5
m³), despite the far lower density of lithic debris north of
Mound R. About two-thirds as many worked pieces of

Table 5.8   Counts and Weights of Greenstone Items from
Sites in the Moundville Area

Site	Worked		Unworked	
	no. wt. (g)		no. wt. (g)	
Moundville, north of Mound R[1]	23	1,170.2	23	48.8
White, late Moundville III refuse deposit[2]	19	55.8	16	15.5
Surface collections, Black Warrior floodplain[3]	38	2,029.3	--[4]	--[4]

[1] From Scarry (1986)
[2] Not included here are 1 whole axhead, 1 broken
   axhead, and 1 discoidal found during the 1930-31
   AMNH excavations.
[3] From Bozeman (1982) and Alexander (1982)
[4] Bozeman (1982) did not distinguish between worked
   and unworked, so all pieces are counted as
   worked; Alexander (1982) only reported worked
   greenstone.

greenstone were found north of Mound R as were found
in complete surface collections of nearly thirty Black
Warrior River valley sites with Mississippian components, and unlike the material north of Mound R, some
of the surface collected material is likely to be of pre-
Mississippian date.

While it is evident that the deposits north of Mound R
have an unusual abundance of greenstone, there is another aspect of this assemblage that is not evident in
table 5.8. The greenstone from north of Mound R in- *workshop*
cludes items that appear to have broken during manufacture, as well as unworked pieces that are of a size
and shape that preclude their being fragments of a
finished object. In other words, greenstone items were
being made north of Mound R. Further evidence of
greenstone manufacture at Moundville is found in the
Roadway collection, which contains three greenstone ax
"preforms." These were chipped to shape, but the process of grinding had only just begun at the time the artifacts were deposited. In their present form, they would
not have been functional axheads. They are clearly tools
in the process of being manufactured.

In contrast, the greenstone pieces from the White site
are either clearly fragments of finished items or unworked chips that are so small that it is likely they also
are fragments of broken items. There is no greenstone
manufacturing debris at the White site. Manufacturing
debris is all but absent from the 1978–79 UMMA surface
collections of other outlying sites, with a couple of large,
unworked pieces from one site (1Ha107A) being the
only examples (T. Bozeman, personal communication;
M. Pope, personal communication). North of Mound R at
Moundville is the only location within the chiefdom *Axes*
where evidence of manufacture has been found, though
greenstone products were widely distributed throughout the chiefdom. Numerically, the most important
greenstone products were axheads. Whole axheads or

fragments of broken axheads are found at all levels of the settlement hierarchy. Spatulate "ceremonial" axes (also called spuds) and small discs (so-called chunkee stones) were also made of greenstone, but these items or fragments thereof have only been found at Moundville and at the single-mound local centers.

Aside from items of chert and greenstone, a variety of other objects made of stone were used during the Moundville period. These include pieces of minerals used for pigments; several kinds of rock used for beads, figurines, and pipes; and a kind of fine-grained sandstone from which most of the circular or rectangular paint palettes were made. Of these lithic items, only the paint palettes could be called tools. Discussion of the other items is deferred until later in this chapter, after the palettes have been discussed.

The artifacts called paint palettes are circular or rectangular, usually finely ground, slabs of fine micaceous sandstone. They are sometimes decorated with incised lines on one or both faces, as for example on the famous "rattlesnake disc" from Moundville (Moore 1905, figure 7; see also Webb and DeJarnette 1942, 287–91). These artifacts often are found with traces of red, white, or black pigment on one or both faces and are therefore thought to be mortars for grinding mineral pigments.

Paint palettes have been found at sites of all levels of the Moundville site hierarchy. At Moundville, they occur in contexts of Moundville I through Moundville III date. At the White site, fragments of a notched-edge, circular sandstone palette with traces of red pigment on both sides were found in the late Moundville III refuse deposit. Fragments of at least three different palettes were also recovered from features at 1Tu459, an early Moundville I farmstead on the Black Warrior floodplain 21 km north of Moundville (L. Michals, personal communication). The locus of manufacture of sandstone palettes is not known, though a distributional study by

Webb and DeJarnette (1942, 287–91) noted that Moundville is the locus of greatest abundance of these items throughout the Southeast. The source(s) of the sandstone is not certain, either. It is possible that the sandstone comes from the Pottsville Formation, which crops out from Tuscaloosa northward (V. Steponaitis, personal communication).

In summary, the lithic technology of the Moundville culture was focused on locally available raw material. All stages of the production of formal, chipped-stone tools took place at the White site, but whether this was the case at the other single-mound sites and/or farmsteads and hamlets is difficult to determine on the basis of the surface collections. Certainly the raw material was equally available to all communities in the chiefdom. The little nonlocal material that was found at White was late-stage manufacturing debris or finished tools. In contrast, in at least one precinct of Moundville (north of Mound R), nonlocal chipped stone was relatively abundant. Furthermore, the nonlocal material in this precinct is primarily debris from early and intermediate stages of manufacturing. Precisely the same relationship between Moundville and the outlying sites holds true for ground-stone tools: only whole or broken ground-stone tools are found at the outlying sites, while manufacturing debris is found in one area (at least) at Moundville.

Other Craft Items

Compared with the cases for pottery and stone tools, there is little available information concerning the production of other craft items. In part, this is due to the nonpreservation of organic materials, but it is also due to the apparently sparse use of durable, formal tools in the production of craft items. While valuable information might be obtained from microscopic use-wear analyses of extensive samples of utilized flakes, this is a task I leave for other researchers. The information already available, however, does suggest a pattern for the production and distribution of other craft items.

A simple way to present information about the distribution of craft items in the Moundville chiefdom is to tabulate the kinds of items found at various sites. Since pottery and stone tools have already been discussed, they are omitted here. Bone tools and all organic materials are also omitted, since their absence at a site is at least as likely to be due to poor preservation as to actual prehistoric distributions. Table 5.9 is a list of the kinds of items recovered from Moundville, while the list of items found at the single-mound sites is presented in table 5.10.

Table 5.9 Selected Artifact Classes Found at Moundville

Copper ax	Mica
Copper knife	Galena
Copper gorget	White (lead) paint
Copper strip	Hematite/red paint
Copper symbol badge	Limonite/yellow paint
Copper sheet pendant	Glauconite/green paint
Copper sheet hair ornament	Psilomelane
Copper beads	Graphite
Copper earspools	Bentonite
Copper fishhooks	White clay
Copper-clad wood and bone	Asphaltum
Other copper	Shark teeth
Stone ceremonial axes	Bear canines
Stone paint palettes	Miscellaneous carnivore teeth
Stone earplugs	Ivory-billed woodpecker beaks
Stone gorgets	Bird claws
Stone ("chunkee") discs	Shell beads
Red stone pendants	Shell earplugs
Amethyst human head	Shell pendants
Ceremonial flint blades	Shell gorgets
Carved stone bowls	Shell spoons
Plain stone pipes	Engraved shell cups
Stone effigy pipes	Conch columellae
Obsidian projectile points	Pearl beads

Table 5.10 Selected Artifact Classes Found at Single-mound
Sites

1Ha7/8 (White)	1Tu46/47[1]	1Tu2[2] (Snows Bend)
Copper ornament	Stone ceremonial	Stone ceremonial
Drilled bear canines	ax	ax
Stone paint palette		Shell beads
Shell pendant		Green paint
Shell beads		
Hematite/red paint		
Limonite/yellow paint		
Galena		
Red stone pendant		

[1] From Bozeman (1982)
[2] From DeJarnette and Peebles (1970)

The locus of manufacture of most of the items in these
two lists is not known. As previously stated, stone axheads and other greenstone items were probably made
north of Mound R at Moundville, and stone palettes may
have been manufactured in west-central Alabama. He-
matite and limonite are locally available throughout the
Moundville chiefdom, and white clay is widespread on
the Fall Line Hills bordering the Black Warrior River
valley. Bear and carnivore teeth, ivory-billed wood-
pecker beaks, and bird claws were also available locally
or at no great distance. Nearly all of the other items in
the list are of nonlocal raw materials, though they are
not necessarily of nonlocal manufacture. For example, a
small pit south of the Conference Building at Moundville
contained 208 g of unworked mica, which appears to be
manufacturing debris. Sources of sheet mica are several
hundred kilometers to the east and northeast, in the
South Appalachian Mountains (Jones 1926, 202–3). Another kind of item probably manufactured at Moundville
is a teardrop-shaped red stone pendant: a fragment of

one that apparently broke during manufacture was found at Moundville in Smithsonian Institution excavations during the nineteenth century (Steponaitis 1983b, 138, figure 10g). The sources (at least two different materials were used) of the red stone are not known, though the materials could well come from Pottsville Formation outcrops north of Tuscaloosa. Shell beads are another craft item possibly manufactured at Moundville, with by-products of bead manufacture being most abundant east of Mound E (Peebles 1978c, 17). In contrast to these items, there is no information about the location of manufacture of artifacts of shark teeth, pearl, copper, shell (other than beads), or rare materials such as amethyst. A thorough reanalysis of the collections from excavations at Moundville might shed light on some of these materials, but as yet there are no plans for such a major undertaking.

The available information concerning production of the items listed in tables 5.9 and 5.10 indicates that all the nonlocal materials demonstrably worked within the Moundville chiefdom were worked only at Moundville. There is *no* evidence for the manufacture of items of nonlocal materials at the outlying sites. Undeniably, the lack of evidence of such craft production at the outlying sites may be due to poor preservation or the limited extent of excavations. However, there is an obvious parallel between the data in the preceding paragraph and the data on the production of stone tools. Regardless of the function, social significance, or symbolic content of items made of nonlocal raw material, if they were made within the Moundville chiefdom, they were made at Moundville itself. Unfortunately, it is difficult to determine the locus of production of most items made from local raw materials. Such items in tables 5.9 and 5.10, as well as objects of cane, wood, bone, fiber, etc., are of a nature such that their manufacture would leave few diagnostic or durable by-products. An unusual abundance (per unit excavated area) of bone awls in the northeast quarter of Moundville has been interpreted as a possible hide-working area (Peebles and Kus 1977, 442); however, differential preservation could also account for this pattern, and it has not been demonstrated that these tools were used as awls rather than, for instance, corn shuckers (C. Peebles, personal communication). For the two classes of goods that would leave durable and distinctive evidence of their manufacture—ceramics and chipped-stone tools—there is good evidence of their manufacture from local raw materials at the outlying sites as well as at Moundville.

Items of Known Nonlocal Manufacture

The principal class of items found within the Moundville chiefdom but known to be of nonlocal manufacture is pottery. We have ample ceramic data from the full range of sites occupied during the Moundville chiefdom. The extensive sherd collections from the outlying sites were analyzed by Bozeman (1982). Steponaitis (1983a, 347–48) identified the nonlocal vessels in the collection of whole pots from Moundville, and I have reported elsewhere (Welch 1989) on the nonlocal ceramics in the Roadway sherd collection. With the addition of the ceramics from the White site excavations, we are thus in a good position to examine the distribution of nonlocal ceramics within the Moundville chiefdom.

Nonlocal ceramics within the Moundville chiefdom include vessels from several locales in the lower Mississippi River valley, central Tennessee, and south Alabama. There are no whole vessels from what is now Georgia or from east of the Apalachicola River in Florida, though the Roadway sherds do include pieces from three or four vessels likely to be of northwest Georgia origin. In the surface collections from outlying sites, no pottery of definite nonlocal manufacture was noted (Bozeman 1982), nor were any nonlocal vessels found with the burials at Snows Bend (DeJarnette and Peebles 1970) or the White site. The 1983 excavations at White also produced no sherds definitely from vessels of nonlocal manufacture, though some sherds are sufficiently unusual in paste characteristics or decoration that they may be from nonlocal vessels. In part, the absence of identified nonlocal vessels outside Moundville may be due to the paucity of whole vessels in the collections; it is easier to identify a whole vessel as being of nonlocal origin than it is to identify a sherd from one. Nevertheless, if nonlocal vessels were present at the outlying sites in the same frequencies as they are in the Moundville whole vessel collection, it is almost certain that at least a few of them would have been identified: Steponaitis classified 935 whole vessels from Moundville, of which 16.3 percent (152) are nonlocal. Nonlocal ceramics in the Roadway sherd collection are scarcer, probably accounting for less than 5 percent of the total ceramics. Nonlocal vessels were also identified in the comparatively small sherd collection from excavations north of Mound R and south of the Conference Building (Steponaitis 1983a, 289–95). It appears that most of the nonlocal vessels that entered the Moundville chiefdom ended their use-life at Moundville.

As with the local whole vessels, most of the nonlocal whole vessels were found in burials. In every case where the sex of the burial associated with a nonlocal vessel is known, the buried individual was female (C. Peebles, personal communication). An obvious interpretation is that these individuals were nonlocal women who married in and brought their native pottery with them. Other interpretations are possible, however, and none of them can be considered more probable than others until tests with independent evidence are produced. The association of nonlocal pots with female burials is clearly a point worthy of future research.

There are a few other items found within the Moundville chiefdom that are known to be, or most likely are, of nonlocal manufacture. The obsidian arrowheads, for instance, probably arrived at Moundville as finished products, though without further information about their morphology, mineralogy, or chemical composition, it is not possible to say where they came from. Galena and graphite, both probably used as pigments, may be regarded as finished products, since it was the material itself that was of value. The nearest graphite sources are in eastern Alabama (Jones 1929), though whether any or all of the graphite at Moundville came from there is not known. Walthall (1981) obtained trace element data for seven pieces of galena from Moundville. Three of the specimens were assigned to the Potosi source in southeastern Missouri, not far from the American Bottom, while the other four specimens apparently came from the Upper Mississippi Valley source in the adjacent portions of Illinois, Wisconsin, and Iowa. Obsidian and graphite have been found only at the Moundville site, while galena has been found at Moundville and two single-mound sites (White and 1Tu50 [Steponaitis, personal communication]). Most of the galena at Moundville are large pieces found in burials, while the galena pieces found at White were found in the refuse deposit and were very small (1.9 g and 0.8 g).

Other artifacts probably of nonlocal manufacture are hoes made of Mill Creek chert from the Shawnee Hills in southwestern Illinois. Substantial numbers of large bifaces made from this material were distributed widely throughout the Midwest during the Mississippian period, almost always in finished form (Cobb 1985). Fragments of Mill Creek chert, some bearing the distinctive hoe-polish, have been found within the Moundville

Table 5.11   Provenience of Mill Creek Chert Hoe
Fragments[1]

No. of fragments	Site	Site type	Moundville phase[2]
1	1Tu56/57	single mound	I
1	1Tu398	single mound	II
1	1Ha91	hamlet	III
2	1Tu259	hamlet	III
1	1Ha14/15	single mound	III
1	1Ha7/8	single mound	III
1	1Tu42/43	single mound	III
1	1Tu2	single mound	III
(multiple)	Moundville	multi-mound	I-III

[1] Information from sites other than 1Ha7/8
   from M. Pope (personal communication)
[2] Phase assignments from Bozeman (1982)

chiefdom; their locations are listed in table 5.11. No
whole hoes have been recovered outside of Moundville,
which could be due either to their rarity or to intensive
curation of the hoes. The paucity of flakes suggests that
Mill Creek hoes were generally scarce at the outlying
sites. Mill Creek hoes, both whole and fragmentary,
have been found at Moundville. As yet, however, too few
of the stone artifacts from Moundville have been examined for any conclusion to be drawn about the abundance or rarity of hoes.

A less-certainly imported set of craft products is engraved shell cups. Excavations by Moore (1905, 1907)
produced several cups and cup fragments, only a few of
which were illustrated in his reports. Steponaitis has recently examined the Moundville artifacts from Moore's
collection, now in the Museum of the American Indian.
A few of the shell pieces have engraving that is
unmistakably similar to engraved shell from the Spiro
site in Oklahoma (Phillips and Brown 1978, 1984). While

the geographic origin of Spiro-style engraving is not definitely known, the remarkable concentration of these engraved shell objects at Spiro suggests that the engravers came from that vicinity. These pieces of engraved shell at Moundville are most likely of Spiroan origin.

An interpretation of the pattern of distribution of nonlocally manufactured items based on the few classes discussed here must be highly tentative. Undoubtedly, there were many other nonlocally manufactured items present within the Moundville chiefdom, but either they have not been identified as such or else they have not preserved or been recovered. It is equally likely that more extensive excavations at the outlying sites would expand the list of nonlocal materials found there. Based on the limited information available, it seems that nonlocal manufacture per se does not affect the pattern of an item's distribution within the chiefdom. Nonlocal ceramics apparently were restricted to the paramount center, galena was present at Moundville and at least one single-mound site, and Mill Creek chert hoes were present in all levels of the settlement hierarchy. The obvious conclusion is that the distribution of nonlocally manufactured items depended on their function and social valuation rather than on their nonlocal origin. I suspect that this conclusion surprises few, if any, of my readers.

The conclusion that the distribution of imports varies from one artifact category to another is noteworthy in one respect. There are some classes of nonlocal goods for which there is no evidence that access to them was controlled by the Moundville paramount. For example, the distribution of Mill Creek hoes provides no grounds for inferring that importation was under the control of the Moundville paramount or other nobility. On the other hand, the distribution of nonlocal vessels lends itself to the inference that there was some restriction on the access to nonlocal pottery (or the women who

brought it?). Similarly, the distribution of galena suggests that it was available to a set of individuals at
Moundville in far greater quantities than it was to the
residents of single-mound sites, and there is no evidence
that it was available to residents of farmsteads and
hamlets. The conclusion stated above, unsurprising
though it is, is an important link in the chain of analysis
by which the pattern of craft production and distribution in the Moundville chiefdom can be reconstructed.

Conclusion

This chapter commenced with a discussion of the limitations on our ability to determine the pattern and organization of craft production in the Moundville chiefdom.
However, the information that is available is, for archaeological data, remarkably consistent. A concise restate-
ment of the conclusions reached above makes this
consistency clear. Ceramics were produced at Moundville, at single-mound sites, and possibly at all levels of
the settlement hierarchy, but at Moundville there was
some degree of specialization in the production of fine-
ware vessels. Chipped-stone tools were made at all levels
of the settlement hierarchy, but the chipping of nonlocal
stone was restricted to Moundville. Ground-stone celts
were distributed throughout the chiefdom, but they
were made only at Moundville. In general, Moundville
was the only site where nonlocal raw materials of any
kind were made into finished products. Most items of
definite or probable nonlocal manufacture were restricted to Moundville, though the distribution of nonlocal goods was conditioned by their function and social
valuation rather than their nonlocal origin. Taking all
this information together, there is little room for doubt
that the Moundville community was both internally specialized in the production of some crafts and quali-

tatively different from other communities in the chiefdom in terms of access to nonlocal raw materials and imported finished products.

The pattern of craft production and distribution in the Moundville chiefdom is one of centralized control of the production of, and access to, most nonutilitarian goods. In contrast, most utilitarian goods were probably produced domestically. Fine-ware vessels and ground-stone celts appear to be exceptions to this generalization. The celts certainly were functional objects, since many of the recovered pieces are impact-chips from the bit. Abrasion and chipping of the bases and lips of fine-ware vessels indicate they also received extensive use before disposal; this usage is not consistent with the vessels' having been made expressly for burial, display, or ceremonial use, which we would expect to be infrequent and careful. It is possible, however, that both the celts and the fine-ware vessels, particularly those made by specialists, may have conveyed prestige as well as being objects of regular domestic use. Aside from celts, the (probably rare) Mill Creek hoes, and at least a few fine-ware vessels, utilitarian items were made of local raw materials and were manufactured at the same sites where they were used. Nonutilitarian items, in contrast, were generally made of nonlocal raw materials, were imported as finished products or were made at Moundville, and were present only at Moundville. The few classes of nonutilitarian items present at single-mound sites were present only in small quantities.

This pattern of craft production and distribution is strongly at odds with the classic redistribution model, in which the production of utilitarian items would be specialized by community. The Moundville data also contrast with the tributary model exemplified by Peebles and Kus's (1977) and Wright's (1977) analysis of Hawaiian economy, in which outlying communities would specialize in the production of nonutilitarian items. The

Moundville case is, rather, a form of prestige goods economy, in which most utilitarian items were produced domestically, most of the utilitarian items not produced domestically were produced at the paramount center, and most nonutilitarian items were produced at and/or restricted to the paramount center.

6 Structure and Operation of Moundville's Economy

Production and Distribution in the Moundville Economy

The pattern of production and distribution of goods in the Moundville chiefdom can be diagrammed in the same way as the economic models described in chapter two. Figure 6.1 depicts the economic structure of the chiefdom, though the complexity of the diagram has been reduced by showing only four local centers, rather than the six actually present in the Moundville III phase. As expected, the observed pattern does not match any of the models perfectly. Nevertheless, the observed pattern very closely resembles the mobilization model for the subsistence sector (see figure 2.2), combined with the prestige goods model for the production and distribution of craft items (see figure 2.4). Briefly, the data on which figure 6.1 is based are as follows. The results of settlement pattern and catchment analyses presented in chapter four are consistent with the mobilization of agricultural foodstuffs to support the elite at Moundville. In the faunal remains from the White site, there is strong evidence for provisioning of choice parts of deer carcasses to the elite at this local center, and by extension, it seems highly probable that elite individuals resident at Moundville would have been similarly provisioned. As detailed in chapter five, there is evidence that

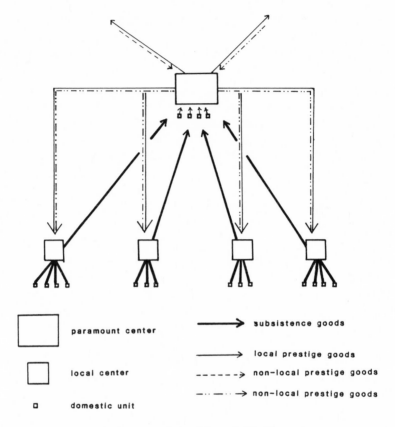

Figure 6.1 The Structure of the Moundville Economy

the centripetal movement of subsistence goods was balanced by the outward distribution of craft items from Moundville. These craft items were primarily objects manufactured nonlocally, or objects manufactured at Moundville from nonlocal raw materials. The outwardly distributed craft items include prestige goods, such as greenstone ceremonial celts and stone paint palettes, as well as objects of apparently utilitarian nature, such as greenstone axes. While the outwardly distributed prestige goods were restricted to the nobility at single-mound sites, the utilitarian goods were available to all segments of the outlying communities. The prestige goods available to the nobility at the single-mound sites constitute only a small subset of the range of prestige goods present at the paramont center. These data are consistent with the prestige goods model of craft production and exchange.

There are also differences between the Moundville economic pattern and the mobilization + prestige goods model. First, no interdistrict exchange of subsistence goods was detected (i.e., the horizontal arrows between local centers in figure 2.2). Since subsistence remains are available for only one of the local centers, the apparent absence of such exchange may be nothing more than an artifact of inadequate sampling. Even if data were available from other local centers, interdistrict exchange might still be difficult to detect. Since the site catchments are so similar, exchanges might have involved subsistence goods that were produced in all districts but that may have been differentially abundant on a seasonal or annual basis.

The second, and more significant, difference between the observed data and the mobilization + prestige goods model is the lack of evidence for the centripetal movement of craft items for the paramount chief to use in external exchange. As discussed in chapter five, this lack of evidence may be due to the lack of preservation of organic materials. Aside from this largely unaddressable issue, there is still a difference between the observed pattern of craft production and the prestige goods model. The paramount center is the only location in the Moundville chiefdom where evidence of craft specialization has been found. In figure 6.1, this is depicted as the production of prestige goods by the domestic units directly beneath the paramount center (the domestic producers are actually resident *in* the paramount center, but drawing the symbols for the producers and their products inside the symbol for the paramount center results in a diagram not easily interpretable). The prestige goods model specifies that craft items destined for exchange are produced throughout the chiefdom and are "passed up as tribute through the political hierarchy to a superordinate chief" (Frankenstein and Rowlands 1978, 77). Frankenstein and Rowlands did describe a variant of the prestige goods model, in which specialized craft production would be centered at the paramount's settlement. They suggested that this would occur where "the technical skill required for the working of certain resources—such as metal—is not accessible to everyone" (Frankenstein and Rowlands 1978, 77–78). The production of greenstone celts and chipped-stone tools from nonlocal raw material certainly does not qualify as the sort of esoteric skill intended in the quoted passage. I also doubt that the mold-making technique of ceramic manufacture used by some potters at Moundville in late Moundville II/Moundville III times qualifies as a technical skill "not accessible to everyone." Certainly, it is not nearly as complex a skill as ore smelting, which is what Frankenstein and Rowlands had in mind. It appears, therefore, that the centralization of craft specialization at the paramount center of the Moundville chiefdom does not coincide with the conditions in which Frankenstein and Rowlands suggest it would develop.

Before proceeding, it is appropriate to call attention to two assumptions that have been made in reconstructing the economic pattern diagrammed in figure 6.1. Most of the data used in this study come from late Moundville III contexts at one local center (the White site) and from late Moundville I contexts north of Mound R at Moundville. The paucity of excavation at other local centers leaves open the possibility that economic relationships between those centers and Moundville may have been different than the relationship between White and Moundville. Surface collections and small-scale excavations at the other local centers provide data that are consistent with the interpretation shown in figure 6.1, but it is an exaggeration to say that these data *support* this interpretation. I have, therefore, assumed that all local centers have similar economic relationships with the paramount center.

The second assumption underlying this reconstruction is that the differences between data from north of Mound R at Moundville and from the White site result from the differences between the social contexts represented by the excavated deposits, rather than from the chronological difference between them. Put simply, I assume there is no change in the economic structure of the chiefdom between late Moundville I and late Moundville III. Where available, data from other contexts at Moundville have also been drawn into the analysis. Many of these data are not well controlled chronologically, and there are no systematically collected and analyzed subsistence remains from Moundville postdating late Moundville I. Moundville was already the paramount center of a complex chiefdom by the time the deposits north of Mound R were formed (Welch 1990), but at present, there is little else to support the assumption of no structural change between late Moundville I and late Moundville III. This fact is of particular importance in regard to the dynamic behavior of the Moundville economy, which is discussed later in this chapter.

External Relations of the Moundville Chiefdom

One aspect of the economy of the Moundville chiefdom has not yet been discussed, namely, the external relations of the chiefdom. By "external relations," I mean the political or other connections manifest by the exchange of goods between polities. Of course, the exchange of goods is not a universal and necessary concomitant of social relationships, but patterns of exchange often are sensitive indicators of such relationships (cf. Sahlins 1972, 185–314).

Information is presented in chapter five about the sources of nonlocal goods present in the Moundville chiefdom. In brief, there are goods from south, west, and north of the Moundville chiefdom, but relatively few that definitely were manufactured to the northeast, east, or southeast.

This pattern is most visible in the imported ceramics. During the period of the Moundville polity's maximum size and complexity (late Moundville II/Moundville III phases), most of what is now Georgia was occupied by communities whose ceramics predominantly had complicated-stamped exteriors (i.e., South Appalachian Mississippian; see Ferguson 1971; Hally and Rudolph 1986). There are no South Appalachian vessels in the collection of whole vessels from Moundville (Steponaitis 1983a). The Roadway excavations at Moundville produced 98,850 sherds, only 24 of them complicated-stamped (Wimberly 1956; Welch 1989). This is well below the estimated abundance of, for example, pottery from the Lower Mississippi Valley (Welch 1989).

On the other hand, there are sources of copper, greenstone, mica, graphite, and conch shell to the northeast, east, or southeast of Moundville, and there are many artifacts made of such materials found within the Moundville chiefdom. It is not clear, however, how many of these artifacts were made elsewhere, and how many were made locally using imported raw materials. Importation of the raw material need not involve exchange, though of course it may do so. Detailed analysis of both extant and new excavation collections at Moundville may clarify the manner in which these objects of nonlocal material came to Moundville.

While researchers have successfully determined the locus of origin of many exotic goods found within the

Moundville chiefdom, there has been much less success in determining where Moundville-manufactured goods went. Aside from pottery, few goods are demonstrably of Moundville manufacture.

One type of item possibly of Moundville manufacture is a triangular pendant made of red stone (see Webb and DeJarnette 1942, plate 58.2; Steponaitis 1983b, figure 10g). A fragmentary pendant similar to the Moundville examples was recovered from the Seven Mile Island site along the Tennessee River in northwest Alabama (Webb and DeJarnette 1942, plate 58.2).

Greenstone axes were manufactured north of Mound R at Moundville, as described in chapter five. Some of these axes may have been exchanged with other polities. Unfortunately, little is understood about the significance of variation in ax morphology, and we cannot yet distinguish where any given ax was made.

Stone paint palettes are another class of items possibly manufactured at Moundville and exchanged extra-locally. Webb and DeJarnette (1942, 287–91) studied the distribution of circular stone palettes in the Southeast and concluded that:

> [it] may be stated with confidence that the vicinity of Moundville, Alabama, has yielded by far the largest number of disks, as well as the largest, most carefully wrought, and most elaborately engraved ones. This would seem to suggest Moundville as a center from which these artifacts spread, although queerly enough it seems to be located on the edge of the area of their known occurrence. It appears that, if Moundville were a center of distribution, they were not carried to the south or east, but that they were confined to the interior drainage basin and to sites reached from the Mississippi River and the Gulf.

If palettes were manufactured at Moundville, it is inter-esting that they have been recovered from northeast

Poss. given-Taker
distinction

Tennessee and northwest Georgia (see Webb and DeJarnette 1942, 290–91). As noted above, these are areas
from which there are very few objects definitely imported to Moundville.

Among the most visible indicators of exchange with
Moundville are ceramic vessels. Nobody has yet attempted to enumerate all the potentially Moundville-
made vessels found outside the Moundville area, and
even the most thorough review of the literature would
not produce definitive results. The difficulty is that at-
tributing a vessel to Moundville-area manufacture is
hazardous unless the person making the attribution is
familiar with the range of pastes, surface finishes, vessel morphologies, decorative motifs, and stylistic treat-
ments of known Moundville vessels and can examine the
vessel in question firsthand.

The situation is not hopeless, however. It has long
been recognized (e.g., Griffin 1939, 163) that some pottery found at sites in north Alabama closely resembles
pottery made at Moundville. In an effort to determine
whether sherds from sites in the Guntersville basin in
northeast Alabama actually came from vessels made at
Moundville, Heimlich (published 1952 but written in
1940–41) submitted Guntersville basin and Moundville
sherds to F. R. Matson, then at the University of Michigan Museum of Anthropology, for thin-section analysis.
The results, excerpted by Heimlich (1952, 29–32), were
inconclusive: a Moundville origin for Guntersville
sherds could not be ruled out, but a local origin was considered more probable. Unfortunately, there have been
no subsequent technical attempts to determine whether
vessels, or sherds from them, found in north Alabama
were actually made at Moundville. Among the published
photographs of north Alabama ceramics, there are a few
vessels that are morphologically and stylistically so similar to Moundville pottery that a Moundville origin for
them is likely. These include vessels of Moundville En-

graved *var. Hemphill* (Webb and DeJarnette 1942, plates 67.1, 262.2, 268.1), Moundville Engraved *var. Tuscaloosa* (Webb and DeJarnette 1942, plates 122.2, 261.1 left, 267.2), and Bell Plain *var. Hale* (Webb and DeJarnette 1942, plate 60.1). Without trace element or thin-section analysis, it is not possible to say whether these pots were made at Moundville or were made elsewhere by potters familiar with Moundville products.

Other vessels potentially of Moundville origin but found elsewhere include a number of those from the lower Mississippi River valley illustrated in Phillips et al. (1951, figures 110a–d, 111f–h). In the captions for these photographs, Phillips et al. carefully distinguish these vessels as "resembling Moundville type," rather than as being imports from Moundville, a caution applauded here. Nearer to the Moundville site, sherds from vessels possibly originating at Moundville have been identified at Lubbub (Mann 1983, 74) along the central Tombigbee River. Doubtless many other sherds of the same sort can be found elsewhere in west Alabama. Continuing research on the collections of the Alabama Department of Archives and History, mostly from the Montgomery area, may reveal vessels from that area that might have been exported from Moundville (C. Sheldon, personal communication). Along the Alabama River from Selma to the Mobile delta—in other words, to the south of Moundville—there seems to have been only sparse occupation during the time of the Moundville chiefdom, and examples of ceramics possibly made at Moundville are correspondingly rare (Jenkins and Paglione 1982, 14–15).

The patterns of identified Moundville imports and exports are mapped in figures 6.2 and 6.3. Obviously, many more imports than exports have been identified. Perhaps surprisingly, there is little obvious symmetry between the two maps; that is, there is little evidence for *reciprocal* exchanges between Moundville and other pol-

1) Reciprocal relationships w/ groups providing finished goods   2) Debtor to groups providing raw materials   3) Creditor to some groups receiving finished goods.

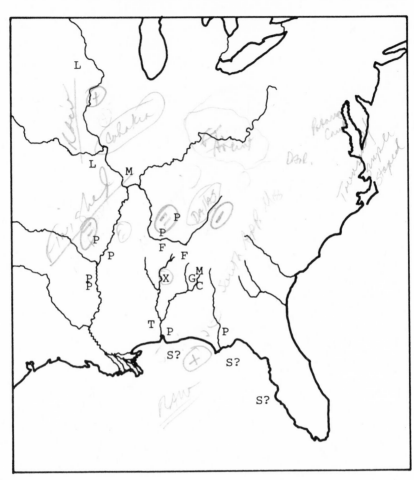

P   Pottery   X   Moundville
M   Mill Creek chert hoes
F   Ft. Payne/Bangor
    chert
T   Tallahatta quartzite/
    Coastal Plain chert
M   Mica
G   Greenstone
L   Galena
S   Marine shell
C   Graphite

Figure 6.2   Location of Origin of Artifacts or Materials Found at
            Moundville

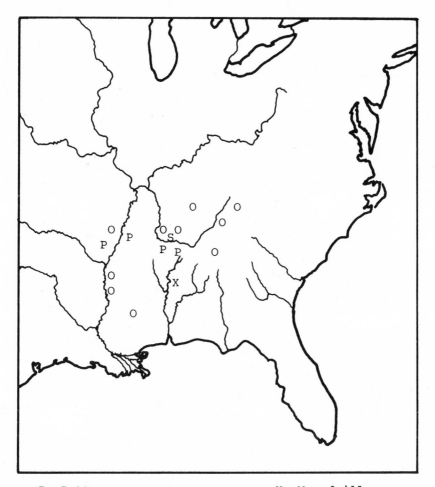

P   Pottery   X   Moundville
O   Paint palettes
S   Red slate pendants

Figure 6.3   Location of Possible Exports from Moundville

ities. It must be kept in mind, however, that these maps
only depict sources and destinations of *durable* artifacts, and that if we were somehow able to add the
sources and destinations of organic craft products,
these maps might look very different. Meanwhile, some

of the patterning of imports and exports is not particularly obvious in these maps.

A pattern emerges from the maps of Moundville imports and exports when we consider the quantity of items involved and distinguish between raw materials and finished products. Quantitatively, the majority of known Moundville exports are found to the north and west. The situation for imports is a little more complex. In terms of items that arrived at Moundville as finished products, the majority of known imports came from the north and west. There is a rough geographic symmetry between these imports and the known exports. In contrast, the sources of imports from the south and east are primarily sources of raw materials, not necessarily the loci of manufacture of these imports. It would be easy to stretch this point too far; in most cases, we simply do not know where items of these raw materials were manufactured into finished products. It would therefore be premature to conclude that Moundville acted as some kind of manufacturing entrepôt, acquiring raw materials from the south and east and exchanging finished goods with polities to the north and west. In order to determine how the Moundville polity fit into the regional network of exchanges, we will have to find out more about the production of items such as shell beads and copper ornaments, found in quantity at Moundville but whose raw material comes from elsewhere. We will also have to know more about the chronology of Moundville's imports and exports.

Dynamics of the Moundville Economy

Finally, we come to the issue I described in chapter two as the reason for doing research on economic structure, namely, investigating the dynamic behavior of the economy. There are two kinds of dynamic behavior, which I call structural change and secular change. Structural change is fundamental change in the organization of the economy, i.e., change in the *ways* persons and groups are interrelated. Secular change refers to change of the particular persons or groups occupying specific structural positions, without any modification of the overall economic structure. In the following paragraphs, I use the economic structure outlined in figure 6.1 as a model and derive from it expectations about the secular and structural behavior of the Moundville economy. I discuss secular change first.

An economy of the "Moundville model" should minimize the extent or rapidity of secular change, at least in comparison with the tributary model described by Wright (1977, 1984). In an economy with the structure I describe, shortfalls in the production of subsistence goods in one or a few districts of the chiefdom would have relatively little effect on the paramount's ability to maintain customary levels of distribution of prestige goods. To make up for shortfalls in the tribute flow from one district, the paramount could temporarily increase the tribute extraction rate for other districts. The paramount could thereby continue to sponsor a stable level of craft production and external exchange. Since the prestige goods desired by the lesser nobility are of nonlocal origin, the paramount's ability to maintain craft production and exchange levels would enable the paramount to supply the nobles' wants unabated. This contrasts with the tributary model presented by Wright (1977, 1984). In an economy of that structure, subsistence shortfalls in even one district can decrease or eliminate the supply of a whole class of craft items, thereby decreasing the paramount's ability to maintain customary levels of external exchange and internal distribution of prestige goods. Of course, an economy of the Moundville model, just like a tributary economy, would be susceptible to political unrest if shortfalls in subsistence production

were general throughout the chiefdom. Insofar as subsistence shortfalls are caused by the vagaries of weather,
the Moundville-model economy is resistant to secular
change except in response to widespread weather phenomena, while a tributary economy is susceptible to secular change as a result of both widespread and localized
weather phenomena.

The structure of the Moundville-model economy
should also minimize the possibility of political unrest
resulting from intentional manipulation of production
at the district level. In a tributary economy, decreased
production rates in a few key districts can seriously im-
pair the incumbent paramount's ability to meet the de-
mand for largess. Intentional manipulation of district
economies is thus an obvious strategy for a potential
usurper of the paramountcy. In contrast, a potential
usurper of the paramountcy in a Moundville-model
chiefdom would have to manipulate the rate of production of subsistence goods in more than a few districts or
would have to manipulate the production of craft items
at the paramount center. Both of these alternatives are
riskier undertakings than would be required of a potential usurper in a tributary economy, since they would be
more difficult to conceal from the paramount.

Another economic strategy for usurping the paramountcy in a Moundville-model chiefdom would be manipulation of external exchange, either by interdicting
travel or by co-opting the external partners in exchanges. Such tactics would also be difficult to conceal
from the paramount, since they would involve long jour-
neys by the potential usurper or movement of a sizable
group of his supporters. In all but the largest of
chiefdoms, it would be an easy matter for the paramount
to determine who is not where they are supposed to be.
Thus secular changes resulting from this sort of economic manipulation should be fairly rare in a chiefdom
of the Moundville model.

Do archaeological data from the Moundville chiefdom fulfill the expectation of a low rate of secular change? This is a difficult question to answer. If usurpation of the paramountcy were followed by a shift of the paramount center, then the rate of secular change could be estimated by the frequency of shifting of the paramount center. In the Moundville chiefdom, however, it is clear that once the Moundville site became the paramount center, it remained so despite whatever secular change may have occurred. Obviously, a part of being the Moundville paramount was being *at* the Moundville site, with its massive public architecture and rich symbolic content. Once the construction of the mound-plaza complex was begun, the Moundville site became a nonportable symbol of the political power and authority of the Moundville paramount, so that prospective Muhammads must needs go to the mounds rather than vice versa. Whether the replacement of one ruling lineage by another might have been physically symbolized in some other way, such as the addition of another layer of mound fill and the erection of new mound-top structures, is an interesting question for which I have no answer. In any case, we have practically no knowledge of the stratigraphy of mounds of Moundville.

In short, I see no good way to estimate the rate of secular change in the Moundville economy. This situation might be improved with the addition of stratigraphic data from the mounds at Moundville, but the real problem is a lack of bridging arguments rather than a lack of data. Until we can determine how to recognize secular economic change in the archaeological record of the Moundville chiefdom, these implications of the structure of the economy will remain intriguing but untested.

In addition to the implications for secular change, the organization of the Moundville economy has implications for its structural dynamics. Knowing how an economy is organized should help the researcher to determine what factors may cause the organization to change. No major factors, such as demographic collapse, environmental catastrophe, and subjugation by more complex societies, appear to have been involved in the collapse of the Moundville chiefdom. Current evidence (see Peebles 1987b) suggests that the collapse was not due to loss of population, territory, or autonomy but was essentially a political collapse.

A distinctive feature of the economic model I describe is that a loss of external exchange should lead to political collapse, as was also pointed out by Frankenstein and Rowlands (1978, 79) in their discussion of the prestige goods model. If the symbols that legitimize the status and authority of the elite become unavailable, then the legitimacy of the elite inevitably will be called into question. If only a few of the symbols become unavailable, it is probable that substitutes can be introduced. However, if a large number of legitimizing symbols are persistently or chronically unavailable, the system of statuses is likely to break down. This leads us to inquire what condition(s) might lead to a breakdown of external exchange.

For a large and powerful chiefdom, unavailability of a large number of legitimizing symbols is not likely to ensue from the loss of only one or two partners in external exchange, but rather from a decline in a paramount's ability to dominate the region. So long as the paramount remains able to dominate neighboring polities militarily, it is to their advantage to maintain peaceful relationships through exchange. If the paramount cannot dominate the neighboring polities, then those polities are free to shift their alliances. If a large number of neighboring polities shift their alliance and cease exchanges with the formerly dominant chiefdom, then the chiefdom as a political entity is likely to collapse. Maintaining effective regional military coercion, then, is the key to maintaining the paramount's position in the regional exchange network and thereby the stability of the status system at home.

There is substantial evidence that the internal political collapse of the Moundville chiefdom was associated with some shift(s) of the regional military balance. Unfortunately, our chronological control of these developments is imprecise. Throughout the Moundville I and II phases (roughly A.D. 1000–1400), the Moundville site had no fortifications. Sometime in the Moundville III phase (probably before A.D. 1500), a bastioned palisade wall was built around the site (Peebles 1986, 29). It was kept in repair, and sections of it were completely rebuilt at least twice (Allan 1982). At (very) roughly the same time as the palisade was erected at Moundville, there were movements of population north and south of the Moundville chiefdom. Based on the presence and absence of ceramic chronological markers in sites of the Pickwick Basin (Webb and DeJarnette 1942) in northwest Alabama, the people who lived there and formerly exchanged goods with Moundville moved out of the area in the late 1400s or early 1500s. To the south of Moundville, there was a major increase of population along the lower and middle Alabama River at roughly the same time (Jenkins and Paglione 1982, 14–15). This may also be the time during which the chiefdom of Coosa rose to regional prominence (Hudson et al. 1985). Of course, change in the regional distribution of population does not necessarily mean that Moundville was losing military dominance. Considering the evidence of palisade construction at Moundville, however, I think it is safe to conclude that *something* about regional political dynamics changed and that the change was probably not in Moundville's favor.

While all this was taking place, the abundance of imported items at Moundville steadily declined. Steponaitis (1989) presented figures for the abundance of various

Table 6.1   Absolute Abundance and Abundance per Dated Burial
of Imported Artifacts in Burials at Moundville[1]

Moundville phase	I		I/II		II	
No. of dated burials	17		41		59	
	no.	no./bu.	no.	no./bu.	no.	no./bu.
Copper						
Earspool	0	-	5	0.12	7	0.12
Gorget/pendant	1	0.06	0	-	2	0.03
Cutouts[2]	0	-	1	0.02	1	0.02
Other ornament	0	-	3	0.07	5	0.08
Axe	0	-	0	-	1	0.02
Fish hook	0	-	3	0.07	0	-
Total	1	0.06	12	0.29	16	0.27
Shell						
Ear plug	0	-	0	-	0	-
Gorget/pendant	0	-	2	0.05	3	0.05
Beads[2]	2	0.12	3	0.07	4	0.07
Other ornament	0	-	4	0.10	1	0.02
Cup	0	-	0	-	1	0.02
Total	2	0.12	9	0.22	9	0.15
Imported vessels	3	0.18	5	0.12	4	0.07

[1] Data from Steponaitis (1989)
[2] Multiple items found with the same burial are counted
    as a single occurrence.

imported goods at Moundville. (Note that Steponaitis's
study is an expansion on the work done by Peebles
[1987a]; Steponaitis's figures are used here because they
are based on more extensive data than Peebles's work.)
Since the items being counted are normally found in
burials, and since the number of burials differs by archaeological phase, Steponaitis standardized the import
abundances by dividing the number of goods by the
number of dated burials per phase. The results are listed
in table 6.1. and are displayed in figure 6.4. All of these
classes of imports are most abundant around the
Moundville I/II phase boundary, and decline in abundance from the start of the Moundville III phase onward.

II/III 222		III 149		III/IV 15		IV 2	
no.	no./bu.	no.	no./bu.	no.	no./bu.	no.	no./bu.
10	0.04	5	0.03	0	-	0	-
4	0.02	3	0.02	0	-	0	-
1	<0.01	0	-	0	-	0	-
4	0.02	4	0.03	0	-	0	-
0	-	1	<0.01	0	-	0	-
0	-	0	-	0	-	0	-
19	0.09	13	0.09	0	-	0	-
1	<0.01	4	0.03	0	-	0	-
6	0.03	3	0.02	0	-	0	-
23	0.10	13	0.09	0	-	0	-
7	0.03	4	0.03	0	-	0	-
0	-	0	-	0	-	0	-
37	0.17	24	0.16	0	-	0	-
26	0.12	10	0.08	0	-	0	-

At the moment, we cannot determine the relative chronological order of these political and economic changes. It is also appropriate to note that the information on import abundances still includes only a portion of the total imported goods, so these figures are only preliminary. In short, this is as far as the data currently can take us. While the data are not inconsistent with the proposition that loss of regional military dominance caused Moundville's collapse, it would be an exaggeration to say that the data supported the proposition.

Conclusion

The economic model outlined in figure 6.1 is a tentative construct, contingent on the available data. Data on

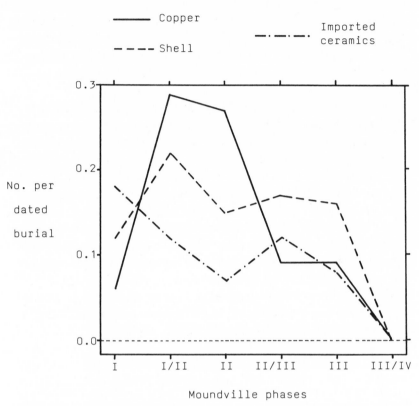

Figure 6.4 Abundance of Selected Imported Goods per Dated Burial at Moundville

consumption of goods at the Moundville site are extensive, though additional data on food procurement and
consumption are desirable. Data on craft production at
Moundville are of uneven quality; thorough restudy of
the extensive collection of artifacts from the site should
improve the current state of affairs. For the single-
mound sites, we have detailed information on production and consumption for only one site, and much more
sketchy information from the others. Our knowledge of
production and consumption at nonmound sites is
slender indeed. We may not have an accurate picture of

activities at these sites until several dozen farmsteads have been excavated. If research stimulated by this study reveals that the picture I present is inaccurate, then my work will have served at least one useful purpose.

Meanwhile, the study of regional political dynamics in the late prehistoric Southeast is in an exciting stage of development. Extensive river basin surveys culminating in the 1970s, combined with advances in our understanding of spatial and temporal variation of artifact styles, have enabled archaeologists to begin assembling comprehensive pictures of regional political dynamics (e.g., Anderson 1987; Hally 1987; Milner 1987; J. Scarry 1987; Williams and Shapiro 1987). In view of the recent, rapid progress made in reconstructing the regional political scene, it would be hubris on my part to regard my interpretations of Moundville's role in the region as the final word on the subject. My efforts are preliminary; I hope the picture soon will be much clearer.

7 Conclusion

As a brief conclusion to this study, I think a review of its limitations and its unanswered questions is appropriate. The model of Moundville's economic organization that I present is an incomplete picture. It is based on current archaeological data, whose limitations I have repeatedly pointed out. The picture is also based on assumptions about the data, such as comparability despite noncontemporaneity. The justifiability of some of these assumptions is admittedly slender. These issues are essentially empirical. My model of Moundville's economy will have to be revised (or even discarded) as further research provides new data. There are, however, more important issues.

The origin of this study was a desire to test extant models of chiefdom economic organization, and in doing so, I present a new model. Do I, therefore, suggest that this new model is the way that all chiefdom economies were organized? The answer is a definite no. I see no reason to believe that the economy of any other polity was structured in the same way that Moundville's economy was. This study shows that it is not appropriate to take the economic models derived from Precontact Polynesia or Bronze Age Germany and apply them to one particular Mississippian society in Alabama. It would be equally inappropriate to expect that the economy of a cattle-herding/millet-farming Iron Age Bantu society would have the same structure as that of a maize-cultivating Mississippian society. The inappropriateness stems not only from the obvious disparity in cultural traditions and staple foods, but also from the fact that different societies have different histories.

Accounting for the different histories of different polities has been a principal focus of research on chiefdoms during the last decade. Prior to that, research had focused on "schemes to classify societies as chiefdoms or not" (Earle 1987, 279). These classification schemes usually linked political and economic criteria (e.g., Service 1971; Peebles and Kus 1977). As Earle's (1987) review shows, researchers more recently have realized that the precise linkages between political structure and economic organization are variable and may account for some of the differences between particular historical sequences. That realization is responsible for the structure of this study: I use economic data as the basis for a model of the economic organization of the Moundville polity, and only then do I examine the linkage between economic organization, political control, and historical development.

While my model of the Moundville economy is more or less securely grounded in archaeological data, my investigation of the linkage between the economy, politics, and history is less secure, less conclusive. The inconclusiveness stems in part from the newness of the questions; sometimes new questions cannot be answered with extant data. In part, however, the inconclusiveness apparent in my discussion of economy, politics, and history stems from methodological problems. How, for instance, can we recognize archaeologically what I call secular change? How do we untangle the web of causality between structural economic change and the regional political fortunes of a chiefdom? While I have made suggestions throughout this study as to goals for new fieldwork, I think it is more important to confront these methodological issues. There, I believe, lies the most important direction for future research.

References Cited

Alexander, Lawrence S.
1982   *Phase I Archaeological Reconnaissance of the Oliver Lock and Dam Project Area, Tuscaloosa, Alabama.* Report of Investigations, no. 33. Tuscaloosa: University of Alabama Office of Archaeological Research.

Allan, Aljean W.
1982   Mound State Monument Palisade Excavations 1978–1982. Paper presented at the 38th Annual Meeting of the Southeastern Archaeological Conference, Memphis, Tennessee.

1983   An Analysis of Lithic Materials from the Lubbub Creek Archaeological Locality. In *Studies of Material Remains from the Lubbub Creek Archaeological Locality,* edited by Christopher S. Peebles, 138–93. Prehistoric Agricultural Communities in West Central Alabama, vol. 2. Report submitted to the U.S. Army Corps of Engineers, Mobile District, by the University of Michigan Museum of Anthropology, Ann Arbor.

Anderson, David G.
1987   Mississippian Political Evolution in the Savannah River Basin. Paper presented at the 44th Annual Meeting of the Southeastern Archaeological Conference, Charleston, South Carolina.

Bogan, Arthur E.
1980   *A Comparison of Late Prehistoric Dallas and Overhill Cherokee Subsistence Strategies in the Little Tennessee River Valley.* Ph.D. diss., University of Tennessee. Ann Arbor: University Microfilms.

Boutton, Thomas W., Mark J. Lynott, James E. Price, and Peter D. Klein
1986   Stable Carbon Isotope Ratios as Indicators of Maize Agriculture in Southeast Missouri and Northeast Arkansas. Paper presented at the 51st Annual Meeting of the Society for American Archaeology, New Orleans, Louisiana.

Bozeman, Tandy K.
1982   *Moundville Phase Communities in the Black Warrior River Valley, Alabama.* Ph.D. diss., University of California, Santa Barbara. Ann Arbor: University Microfilms.

Broida, Mary
1984   An Estimate of the Percents of Maize in the Diets of Two Kentucky Fort Ancient Villages. In *Late Prehistoric Research in Kentucky,* edited by David Pollack, Charles Hockensmith, and Thomas Sanders, 68–83. Frankfort: Kentucky Heritage Council.

Caddell, Gloria M.
1983   Floral Remains from the Lubbub Creek Archaeological Locality. In *Studies of Material Remains from the Lubbub Creek Archaeological Locality,* edited by Christopher S. Peebles, 194–271. Prehistoric Agricultural Communities in West Central Alabama, vol. 2. Report submitted to the U.S. Army Corps of Engineers, Mobile District, by the University of Michigan Museum of Anthropology, Ann Arbor.

Cambron, James W., and David C. Hulse
1975   *Handbook of Alabama Archaeology, Part I: Point Types.* Birmingham: Archaeological Research Association of Alabama.

Carneiro, Robert L.
1981   The Chiefdom: Precursor of the State. In *The Transition to Statehood in the New World,* edited by Grant D. Jones and Robert R. Kautz, 37–79. New York: Cambridge University Press.

Chmurny, William
1973   *The Ecology of the Middle Mississippian Occupation of the American Bottom.* Ph.D. diss., Univer-

sity of Illinois. Ann Arbor: University Microfilms.

Clarke, Otis M.
1966   *Clay and Shale of Northwestern Alabama.* Geological Survey of Alabama, Circular 20-B, University, Alabama.
1970   *Clays of Southwestern Alabama.* Geological Survey of Alabama, Circular 20-E, University, Alabama.

Cleveland, W. S., and R. McGill
1985   Graphical Perception and Graphical Methods for Analyzing Scientific Data. *Science* 229:828–33.

Cobb, Charles
1985   A Model for the Organization of Production of the Mill Creek Chert Biface Industry. Paper presented at the 50th Annual Meeting of the Society of American Archaeology, Denver, Colorado.

Curren, Cailup
1982   The Alabama River Phase: A Review. In *Archaeology of Southwestern Alabama: A Collection of Papers,* edited by Cailup Curren, 103–32. Camden, Alabama: Alabama Tombigbee Regional Commission.
1984   *The Protohistoric Period in Central Alabama.* Camden, Alabama: Alabama Tombigbee Regional Commission.

Dalton, George
1961   Economic Theory and Primitive Society. *American Anthropologist* 63:1–25.

DeJarnette, David L., and Christopher S. Peebles
1970   The Development of Alabama Archaeology: The Snow's Bend Site. *Journal of Alabama Archaeology* 16:77–119.

Drennan, Richard
1975   *Fabrica San Jose and Middle Formative Society in the Valley of Oaxaca, Mexico.* Ph.D. diss., University of Michigan. Ann Arbor: University Microfilms.

Drennan, Richard, and Carlos Uribe (editors)
1987   *Chiefdoms in the Americas.* Lanham, Maryland: University Press of America.

Earle, Timothy K.
1977   A Reappraisal of Redistribution: Complex Hawaiian
        Chiefdoms. In *Exchange Systems in Prehistory,* ed-
        ited by Timothy K. Earle and Jonathan Ericson,
        213–29. Orlando: Academic Press.
1978   *Economic and Social Organization of a Complex
        Chiefdom: The Halelea District, Kaua'i, Hawaii.* An-
        thropological Paper, no. 63. Ann Arbor: University
        of Michigan Museum of Anthropology.
1987   Chiefdoms in Archaeological and Ethnohistorical
        Perspective. *Annual Review of Anthropology*
        16:279–308.
1989   The Evolution of Chiefdoms. *Current Anthropology*
        30:84–88.

Edwards, M. J., B. H. Williams, A. L. Gray, C. H. Wonser,
M. E. Stephens, and M. E. Swann
1939   *Soil Survey of Hale County, Alabama.* U.S. Depart-
        ment of Agriculture Bureau of Chemistry and Soils
        and the Alabama Department of Agriculture and
        Industries. Washington, D.C.: U.S. Government
        Printing Office.

Ensor, H. Blaine
1981   *Classification and Synthesis of the Gainesville Lake
        Area Lithic Materials: Chronology, Technology, and
        Use.* Archaeological Investigations in the Gaines-
        ville Lake Area of the Tennessee-Tombigbee Water-
        way, vol. 3. Report of Investigations, no. 13.
        Tuscaloosa: University of Alabama Office of Archae-
        ological Research.

Fairbanks, Charles
1979   The Function of Black Drink among the Creeks. In
        Black Drink: A Native American Tea, edited by
        Charles M. Hudson, 120–49. Knoxville: University
        of Tennessee Press.

Feinman, Gary, and Jill Neitzel
1984   Too Many Types: An Overview of Sedentary Pre-
        state Societies in the Americas. *Advances in Archae-
        ological Method and Theory* 7:39–102.

Ferguson, Leland G.
1971   *South Appalachian Mississippian*. Ph.D. diss., University of North Carolina, Chapel Hill.

Firth, Raymond
1965   *Primitive Polynesian Economy*. New York: Norton.

Flannery, Kent V.
1972   The Cultural Evolution of Civilizations. *Annual Review of Ecology and Systematics* 3:399–426.

Forde, Daryll, and Mary Douglas
1967   Primitive Economics. In *Tribal and Peasant Economies*, edited by George Dalton, 13–28. Austin: University of Texas Press.

Frankenstein, Susan, and Michael J. Rowlands
1978   The Internal Structure and Regional Context of Early Iron Age Society in Southwestern Germany. *University of London Institute of Archaeology Bulletin* 15:73–112.

Fried, Morton H.
1967   *The Evolution of Political Society*. New York: Random House.

Fusfeld, Daniel
1957   Economic Theory Misplaced: Livelihood in Primitive Society. In *Trade and Market in Early Empires*, edited by Karl Polanyi, Conrad M. Arensburg, and Harry W. Pearson, 342–56. Chicago: Henry Regnery.

Gilbert, B. Miles
1980   *Mammalian Osteology*. Laramie, Wyoming: Modern Printing.

Gipson, P. S.
1978   Coyotes and Related *Canis* in the Southeastern United States with a Comment on Mexican and Central American *Canis*. In *Coyotes: Biology, Behavior, and Management*, edited by Marc Bekoff, 191–209. Orlando: Academic Press.

Griffin, James B.
1939   Report on the Ceramics of Wheeler Basin. In *An Archaeological Survey of Wheeler Basin on the Tennessee River in Northern Alabama*, by William S. Webb, 127–65. Bulletin 122. Washington, D.C.: Bureau of American Ethnology.

Haddy, Alice, and Albert Hanson
    1981   Relative Dating of Moundville Burials. *Southeastern Archaeological Conference Bulletin* 24:97–99.

Hally, David
    1987   Platform Mounds and the Nature of Mississippian Chiefdoms. Paper presented at the 44th Annual Meeting of the Southeastern Archaeological Conference, Charleston, South Carolina.

Hally, David, and James L. Rudolph
    1986   *Mississippi Period Archaeology of the Georgia Piedmont.* University of Georgia Laboratory of Archaeology Series, no. 24, Athens.

Hardin, Margaret
    1979   Recommendations for a Comparative Stylistic Analysis of Lubbub and Moundville Ceramics: Implications of the Evidence for Distinct Complex-Traditions and Craft Standardization at Moundville. Ms. in possession of the author.
    1981   The Identification of Individual Style on Moundville Engraved Vessels: A Preliminary Note. *Southeastern Archaeological Conference Bulletin* 24:108–10.

Harper, Roland M.
    1943   *Forests of Alabama.* Geological Survey of Alabama, Monograph 10, University, Alabama.
    1944   *Preliminary Report on the Weeds of Alabama.* Geological Survey of Alabama, Bulletin 53, University, Alabama.

Heimlich, Marion D.
    1952   *Guntersville Basin Pottery.* Geological Survey of Alabama, Museum Paper 32, University, Alabama.

Helms, Mary
    1979   *Ancient Panama: Chiefs in Search of Power.* Austin: University of Texas Press.

Hu, Shiu Ying
    1979   The Botany of Yaupon. In *Black Drink: A Native American Tea,* edited by Charles M. Hudson, 10–39. Knoxville: University of Tennessee Press.

Hudson, Charles, Marvin T. Smith, David J. Hally, Richard Polhemus, and Chester B. DePratter
  1985   Coosa: A Chiefdom in the Sixteenth-Century Southeastern United States. *American Antiquity* 50:723–37.
Jackson, H. Edwin
  1986   *Sedentism and Hunter-Gatherer Adaptations in the Lower Mississippi Valley: Subsistence Strategies during the Poverty Point Period.* Ph.D. diss., University of Michigan. Ann Arbor: University Microfilms.
Jenkins, Ned J.
  1981   *Gainesville Lake Area Ceramic Description and Chronology.* Archaeological Investigations in the Gainesville Lake Area of the Tennessee-Tombigbee Waterway, vol. 2. Report of Investigations, no. 12. Tuscaloosa: University of Alabama Office of Archaeological Research.
Jenkins, Ned J., and H. Blaine Ensor
  1981   *The Gainesville Lake Area Excavations.* Archaeological Investigations in the Gainesville Lake Area of the Tennessee-Tombigbee Waterway, vol. 1. Report of Investigations, no. 11. Tuscaloosa: University of Alabama Office of Archaeological Research.
Jenkins, Ned J., and Jerry J. Nielsen
  1974   *Archaeological Salvage Investigations at the West Jefferson Steam Plant Site.* Report submitted to Alabama Power Co., copy on file at Mound State Monument, Moundville, Alabama.
Jenkins, Ned J., and Teresa L. Paglione
  1982   Lower Alabama River Ceramic Chronology: A Tentative Assessment. In *Archaeology in Southwest Alabama: A Collection of Papers,* edited by Cailup Curren, 5–18. Camden, Alabama: Alabama Tombigbee Regional Commission.
Johnson, Kenneth W.
  1981   *Soil Survey of Tuscaloosa County, Alabama.* U.S. Department of Agriculture Soil Conservation Service, Alabama Agricultural Experiment Station, and Alabama Department of Agriculture and Indus-

tries. Washington, D.C.: U.S. Government Printing Office.

Jones, Walter B.

1926   *Index to the Mineral Resources of Alabama.* Geological Survey of Alabama, Bulletin 28, University, Alabama.

1929   Summary Report on Graphite in Alabama. Geological Survey of Alabama, Circular 9, University, Alabama.

1939   Geology of the Tennessee Valley Region of Alabama. In *An Archaeological Survey of Wheeler Basin on the Tennessee River in Northern Alabama,* by William S. Webb, 9–20. Washington, D.C.: Bureau of American Ethnology.

n.d.   Master Plan Report to Accompany Master Plan for Mound State Monument, Moundville, Alabama. Ms. on file at Mound State Monument, Moundville, Alabama.

Jones, Walter B., and David L. DeJarnette

n.d.   *Moundville Culture and Burial Museum.* Geological Survey of Alabama, Museum Paper 13, University, Alabama.

Klein, Jeffrey, J. C. Lerman, P. E. Damon, and E. K. Ralph

1982   Calibration of Radiocarbon Dates. *Radiocarbon* 24:103–50.

Knight, Vernon J., Jr.

1982   Document and Literature Review. In *Phase I Archaeological Reconnaissance of the Oliver Lock and Dam Project Area, Tuscaloosa, Alabama,* edited by Lawrence S. Alexander, 27–102. Report of Investigations, no. 33. Tuscaloosa: University of Alabama Office of Archaeological Research.

Lopinott, Mark

1984   *Archaeobotanical Formation Processes and Late Middle Archaic Human-Plant Interrelationships in the Midcontinental U.S.A.* Ph.D. diss., University of Southern Illinois, Carbondale. Ann Arbor: University Microfilms.

Lyman, R. Lee

1985   Bone Density and Differential Survivorship in Fossil Classes. *Journal of Anthropological Archae-ology* 3:259–99.

Mann, C. Baxter
1983   Classification of Ceramics from the Lubbub Creek Archaeological Locality. In *Studies of Material Remains from the Lubbub Creek Archaeological Locality,* edited by Christopher S. Peebles, 2–137. Prehistoric Agricultural Communities in West Central Alabama, vol. 2. Report submitted to the U.S. Army Corps of Engineers, Mobile District, by the University of Michigan Museum of Anthropology, Ann Arbor.

McKenzie, Douglas
1964   *The Moundville Phase and Its Position in Southeastern Prehistory.* Ph.D. diss., Harvard University, Cambridge.
1965   The Burial Complex of the Moundville Phase, Alabama. *The Florida Anthropologist* 18:161–73.
1966   A Summary of the Moundville Phase. *Journal of Alabama Archaeology* 12:1–58.

Merrill, William
1979   The Beloved Tree: *Ilex vomitoria* among the Indians of the Southeast and Adjacent Regions. In *Black Drink: A Native American Tea,* edited by Charles M. Hudson, 40–82. Knoxville: University of Tennessee Press.

Michals, Lauren
1981   The Exploitation of Fauna during the Moundville I Phase at Moundville. *Southeastern Archaeological Conference Bulletin* 24:91–93.

Milner, George
1987   The Development and Dissolution of an Organizationally Complex Mississippian Period Culture in the American Bottom, Illinois. Paper presented at the 44th Annual Meeting of the Southeastern Archaeological Conference, Charleston, South Carolina.

Mistovich, Tim S.
1986   *Excavations at Sites 1Tu265 and 1Tu423, Oliver Lock and Dam, Tuscaloosa, Alabama.* Report of In-

vestigations, no. 51. Tuscaloosa: University of Alabama Office of Archaeological Research.

1987   *The Mill Creek Site, 1Tu265, Black Warrior River, Alabama.* Report of Investigations, no. 54. Tuscaloosa: University of Alabama Office of Archaeological Research.

Moore, Clarence B.

1905   Certain Aboriginal Remains of the Black Warrior River. *Journal of the Academy of Natural Sciences of Philadelphia* 13:124–244.

1907   Moundville Revisited. *Journal of the Academy of Natural Sciences of Philadelphia* 13:334–405.

Muller, Jon J.

1984   Mississippian Specialization and Salt. *American Antiquity* 49:489–507.

1986   Pans and a Grain of Salt: Mississippian Specialization Revisited. *American Antiquity* 51:405–8.

Nielsen, Jerry J., John W. O'Hear, and Charles W. Moorehead

1973   *An Archaeological Survey of Hale and Greene Counties, Alabama.* Report submitted to the Alabama Historical Commission, copy on file at Mound State Monument, Moundville, Alabama.

Oberg, Kalervo

1955   Types of Social Structure among the Lowland Tribes of South and Central America. *Amercian Anthropologist* 57:472–87.

Parmalee, P. W., A. Paloumpis, and N. Wilson

1972   *Animals Utilized by Woodland Peoples Occupying the Apple Creek Site, Illinois.* Report of Investigations, no. 23. Springfield: Illinois State Museum.

Peebles, Christopher S.

1971   Moundville and Surrounding Sites: Some Structural Considerations of Mortuary Practices. In *Approaches to the Social Dimension of Mortuary Practices,* edited by James A. Brown, 68–91. Society for American Archaeology, Memoir 15.

1972   Monothetic-Divisive Analysis of the Moundville Burials: An Initial Report. *Newsletter of Computer Archaeology* 8:1–13.

1974   *Moundville: The Organization of a Prehistoric Com-*

munity and Culture. Ph.D. diss., University of California, Santa Barbara. Ann Arbor: University Microfilms.

1978a   Determinants of Settlement Size and Location in the Moundville Phase. In *Mississippian Settlement Patterns,* edited by Bruce Smith, 369–416. New York: Academic Press.

1978b   Moundville: The Form and Content of a Mississippian Society. Ms. in possession of the author.

1978c   Prehistoric Adaptation and Social Organization at Moundville, Alabama. Grant proposal submitted to the National Science Foundation, Washington, D.C.

1979   *Excavations at Moundville, 1905–1951.* Ann Arbor: University of Michigan Press.

1981   Archaeological Research at Moundville: 1840–1980. *Southeastern Archaeological Conference Bulletin* 24:77–81.

1986   Paradise Lost, Strayed, and Stolen: Prehistoric Social Devolution in the Southeast. In *The Burden of Being Civilized: An Anthropological Perspective on the Discontents of Civilization,* edited by Miles Richardson and Malcolm C. Webb, 24–40. Southern Anthropological Society Proceedings, no. 18.

1987a   Moundville from A.D. 1000 to 1500 as Seen from A.D. 1840 to 1985. In *Chiefdoms in the Americas,* edited by Robert Drennan and Carlos Uribe, 21–41. Lanham, Maryland: University Press of America.

1987b   The Rise and Fall of the Mississippian in Western Alabama: The Moundville and Summerville Phases, A.D. 1000 to 1600. *Mississippi Archaeology* 22:1–31.

Peebles, Christopher S. (editor)

1983a   *Excavations in the Lubbub Creek Archaeological Locality.* Prehistoric Agricultural Communities in West Central Alabama, vol. 1. Report submitted to the U.S. Army Corps of Engineers, Mobile District, by the University of Michigan Museum of Anthropology, Ann Arbor.

1983b   *Studies of Material Remains from the Lubbub Creek Archaeological Locality.* Prehistoric Agricultural

Communities in West Central Alabama, vol. 2. Report submitted to the U.S. Army Corps of Engineers, Mobile District, by the University of Michigan Museum of Anthropology, Ann Arbor.

1983c *Basic Data and Data Processing in the Lubbub Creek Archaeological Locality.* Prehistoric Agricultural Communities in West Central Alabama, vol. 3. Report submitted to the U.S. Army Corps of Engineers, Mobile District, by the University of Michigan Museum of Anthropology, Ann Arbor.

Peebles, Christopher S., and Susan M. Kus
1977 Some Archaeological Correlates of Ranked Societies. *American Antiquity* 42:421–48.

Peirce, L. B.
1962 *Surface Water in Tuscaloosa County, Alabama.* Geological Survey of Alabama, County Report 9, University, Alabama.

Phillips, Phillip, and James A. Brown
1978 *Pre-Columbian Shell Engravings from the Craig Mound at Spiro, Oklahoma,* part 1. Cambridge: Peabody Museum Press.

1984 *Pre-Columbian Shell Engravings from the Craig Mound at Spiro, Oklahoma,* part 2. Cambridge: Peabody Museum Press.

Phillips, Phillip P., James A. Ford, and James B. Griffin
1951 *Archaeological Survey in the Lower Mississippi Alluvial Valley, 1940–1947.* Papers of the Peabody Museum of American Archaeology and Ethnology, no. 25. Cambridge: Harvard University.

Polanyi, Karl
1957a The Economy as Instituted Process. In *Trade and Market in Early Empires,* edited by Karl Polanyi, Conrad M. Arensburg, and Harry W. Pearson, 243–69. Chicago: Henry Regnery.

1957b *The Great Transformation.* Boston: Beacon Press.

Pope, Melody K.
1989 *Microtools from the Black Warrior Valley: Technology, Use, and Context.* Master's thesis, State University of New York, Binghamton.

Powell, Mary Lucas
1984   Patterned Associations between Social Rank and Skeletal Pathology at Moundville. Paper presented at the 41st Annual Meeting of the Southeastern Archaeological Conference, Pensacola, Florida.
1988   *Status and Health in Prehistory: A Case Study of the Moundville Chiefdom.* Washington, D.C.: Smithsonian Institution Press.
Richards, Audrey I.
1961   *Land, Labour, and Diet in Northern Rhodesia.* Oxford: Oxford University Press.
Rose, Jerome, and Murray K. Marks
1985   Bioarchaeology and Subsistence in the Central and Lower Mississippi Valley. Paper presented at the 42nd annual meeting of the Southeastern Archaeological Conference, Birmingham, Alabama.
Rowe, R. W., W. G. Smith, and C. S. Waldrop
1912   Soil Survey of Hale County, Alabama. In *Field Operations of the Bureau of Soils, 1909,* 677–703. U.S. Department of Agriculture, report 11, Washington, D.C.
Sahlins, Marshall D.
1958   *Social Stratification in Polynesia.* American Ethnological Society, Monograph 29.
1962   *Moala: Culture and Nature on a Fijian Island.* Ann Arbor: University of Michigan Press.
1972   *Stone Age Economics.* Chicago: Aldine.
Sanders, William T., and Barbara J. Price
1968   *Mesoamerica: The Evolution of a Civilization.* New York: Random House.
Scarry, John
1987   Political Change in the Apalachee Chiefdom: Centralization, Decentralization and Social Reproduction. Paper presented at the 44th Annual Meeting of the Southeastern Archaeological Conference, Charleston, South Carolina.
Scarry, Margaret M.
1981a   Plant Procurement Strategies in the West Jefferson and Moundville I Phases. *Southeastern Archaeological Conference Bulletin* 24:94–96.

1981b   The University of Michigan Moundville Excavations: 1978–1979. *Southeastern Archaeological Conference Bulletin* 24:87–90.

1986   *Change in Plant Procurement and Production during the Emergence of the Moundville Chiefdom.* Ph.D. diss., University of Michigan. Ann Arbor: University Microfilms.

Schoeninger, Margaret, and Christopher S. Peebles

1981   Notes on the Relationship between Social Status and Diet at Moundville. *Southeastern Archaeological Conference Bulletin* 24:96–97.

Scott, Susan L.

1981   Economic and Organizational Aspects of Deer Procurement during the Late Prehistoric Period. Paper presented at the 38th Annual Meeting of the Southeastern Archaeological Conference, Asheville, North Carolina.

1982   Yarborough Site Faunal Remains. In *Archaeological Investigations at the Yarborough Site (22Cl814), Clay County, Mississippi,* by Carlos Solis and Richard Walling, 140–52. Report of Investigations, no. 30. Tuscaloosa: University of Alabama Office of Archaeological Research.

1983   Analysis, Synthesis, and Interpretation of Faunal Remains from the Lubbub Creek Archaeological Locality. In *Studies of Material Remains from the Lubbub Creek Archaeological Locality,* edited by Christopher S. Peebles, 274–381. Prehistoric Agricultural Communities in West Central Alabama, vol. 2. Report submitted to the U.S. Army Corps of Engineers, Mobile District, by the University of Michigan Museum of Anthropology, Ann Arbor.

1984   Analysis of Faunal Remains Recovered at the Ruckers Bottom Site (9EB91), Elbert County, Georgia. In *Prehistoric Human Ecology along the Upper Savannah River: Excavations at the Ruckers Bottom, Abbeville, and Bullard Site Groups,* assembled by David G. Anderson and Joseph Schuldenrein, 639–64. Report submitted to the U.S. Department of Interior National Park Service, Archaeological

Services Branch, Atlanta, by Commonwealth Associates, Jackson, Michigan.

Service, Elman R.

1971 *Primitive Social Organization: An Evolutionary Perspective.* 2d ed. New York: Random House.

1975 *Origins of the State and Civilization: The Process of Cultural Evolution.* New York: Norton.

Sheldon, Craig T.

1974 *The Mississippian-Historic Transition in Central Alabama.* Ph.D. diss., University of Oregon. Ann Arbor: University Microfilms.

Smith, Bruce D.

1975 *Middle Mississippian Exploitation of Animal Populations.* Anthropological Paper no. 57. Ann Arbor: University of Michigan Museum of Anthropology.

Solis, Carlos, and Richard Walling

1982 *Archaeological Investigations at the Yarborough Site (22Cl814), Clay County, Mississippi.* Report of Investigations, no. 30. Tuscaloosa: University of Alabama Office of Archaeological Research.

Spillius, James

1957 Natural Disaster and Political Crisis in a Polynesian Society: An Exploration of Operational Research. *Human Relations* 10:3–28, 113–26.

Steponaitis, Vincas P.

1978 Location Theory and Complex Chiefdoms: A Mississippian Example. In *Mississippian Settlement Patterns,* edited by Bruce D. Smith, 417–53. New York: Academic Press.

1980 Some Preliminary Chronological and Technological Notes on Moundville Pottery. *Southeastern Archaeological Conference Bulletin* 22:46–51.

1983a *Ceramics, Chronology, and Community Patterns: An Archaeological Study at Moundville.* New York: Academic Press.

1983b The Smithsonian Institution's Investigations at Moundville in 1869 and 1882. *Midcontinental Journal of Archaeology* 8:127–60.

1989 Contrasting Patterns of Mississippian Development. Paper presented at a seminar, "Chiefdoms: Their Evolutionary Significance," held at the

School of American Research, Santa Fe, New Mexico.

Steward, Julian H., and Louis C. Faron
1959   *Native Peoples of South America.* New York: McGraw-Hill.

Swanton, John R.
1911   *Indian Tribes of the Lower Mississippi Valley and Adjacent Coast of the Gulf of Mexico.* Bulletin 43. Washington, D.C.: Bureau of American Ethnology.
1946   *The Indians of the Southeastern United States.* Bulletin 137. Washington, D.C.: Bureau of American Ethnology.

Taylor, Donna
1975   *Some Locational Aspects of Middle-Range Hierarchical Societies.* Ph.D. diss., City University of New York. Ann Arbor: University Microfilms.

Thurnwald, Richard
1932   *Economics in Primitive Communities.* Oxford: Oxford University Press.

van der Leeuw, Sander
1979   Analysis of Moundville Phase Ceramic Technology. Ms. in possession of the author.
1981   Preliminary Report on the Analysis of Moundville Phase Ceramic Technology. *Southeastern Archaeological Conference Bulletin* 24:105–8.

Walthall, John A.
1980   *Prehistoric Indians of the Southeast: Archaeology of Alabama and the Middle South.* University: University of Alabama Press.
1981   Galena and Aboriginal Trade in Eastern North America. *Illinois State Museum Scientific Papers,* vol. 17, Springfield.

Webb, William S., and David L. DeJarnette
1942   *An Archaeological Survey of Pickwick Basin in the Adjacent Portions of the States of Alabama, Mississippi, and Tennessee.* Bulletin 129. Washington, D.C.: Bureau of American Ethnology.

Welch, Paul D.
1983   Research at a Moundville Phase Subsidiary Site. Paper presented at the 40th Annual Meeting of the

Southeastern Archaeological Conference, Columbia, South Carolina.

1986   *Models of Chiefdom Economy: Prehistoric Moundville as a Case Study.* Ph.D. diss., University of Michigan. Ann Arbor: University Microfilms.

1989   Chronological Markers and Imported Items from the Roadway Excavations at Moundville. Paper presented at the 46th Annual Meeting of the Southeastern Archaeological Conference, Tampa, Florida.

1990   Mississippian Emergence in West Central Alabama. In *The Mississippian Emergence,* edited by Bruce D. Smith. Washington: Smithsonian Institution Press. In press.

Whalen, Michael

1976   *Excavations at Santo Domingo Tomaltepec: Evolution of a Formative Community in the Valley of Oaxaca, Mexico.* Ph.D. diss., University of Michigan. Ann Arbor: University Microfilms.

Williams, Mark, and Gary Shapiro

1987   The Changing Contexts of Oconee Valley Political Power. Paper presented at the 44th Annual Meeting of the Southeastern Archaeological Conference, Charleston, South Carolina.

Wimberly, Steve B.

1956   A Review of Moundville Pottery. *Southeastern Archaeological Conference Newsletter* 5(1):17–20.

Winston, R. A., W. J. Latimer, L. Cantrell, W. E. Wilkinson, and A. C. McGehee

1914   Soil Survey of Tuscaloosa County, Alabama. In *Field Operations of the Bureau of Soils, 1911,* 5–74. U.S. Department of Agriculture, report 13, Washington, D.C.

Wright, Henry T.

1977   Recent Research on the Origin of the State. *Annual Review of Anthropology* 6:379–97.

1984   Prestate Political Formations. In *On the Evolution of Complex Societies: Essays in Honor of Harry Hoijer, 1982,* edited by Timothy Earle, 41–78. Malibu, California: Undena Publications.

Yarnell, Richard, and Jean Black
    1985   Temporal Trends Indicated by a Survey of Archaic
            and Woodland Plant Food Remains from South-
            eastern North America. *Southeastern Archaeology*
            4:93–106.
Yerkes, Richard W.
    1986   Licks, Pans, and Chiefs: A Comment on "Mississip-
            pian Specialization and Salt." *American Antiquity*
            51:402–4.

Index

Access to resources, 79, 80, 104–10, 132, 135, 136, 177
Acorns, 108, 124, 125. *See also* Oak
Africa, 8, 11
African chiefdoms, 11, 13
Agriculture, 3, 11, 26, 104, 114–32 passim
Alabama Museum of Natural History, 28, 36, 37, 40, 42, 48, 51, 52, 115, 116, 118, 147
Alabama River, 195
Alabama River Appliqué, 52
Alabama River Incised, 47, 52
Alexander, Lawrence, 29
Allan, Aljean, 44, 151, 195
Ambiguity in the ethnographic and ethnohistoric record, 13, 14
American Bottom, 173
Amethyst, 168, 170
Amphibian, 83, 84
Anderson, David, 199
Apalachicola River, 171
Archaeological site survey, 28, 29, 31, 115
Archaic, 162
Army, 12
Arrowheads. *See* Projectile points
Artisan, 134, 139, 148
Ascriptive social ranking, 2, 56–57

Asphaltum, 168
Authority, 8, 193, 194
Awls, 171

Bald cypress *(Taxodium distichum)*, 26, 109
Bangor chert, 155, 161–63
Barton Incised *var. Big Prairie,* 52
Basketry, 135
Bear *(Ursus)*, 88, 132, 168
Beaver *(Castor)*, 85, 87
Behavior, 5, 183
Bell Plain *var. Hale,* 46–49, 54, 187
Bemba, 8, 13
Berries, 110
Birds, 82, 85, 87, 132, 168
Black Belt, 25, 26, 104
Black drink, 113
Black gum *(Nyssa sylvatica)*, 26, 109, 111
Black Warrior River, 23–28, 34, 35, 68, 74, 104, 105, 116, 117, 136
Bone tools, 135, 171
Boutton, Thomas, 115
Bozeman, Tandy, 27, 29–31, 36, 39, 46, 104, 105, 107, 115, 116, 118, 119, 121, 150, 164, 165, 169, 171, 172, 174
Bridewealth, 18

Tributary: model, 16–18, 134, 177, 191; polity, 16
Tribute, 8, 14, 16–18, 121, 182, 191
Tubers, 110
Turkey *(Meleagris gallopavo),* 85, 87
Turtle, 77, 82, 87
Tuscaloosa, 28, 121, 135, 167, 170

Utensils, 11, 134, 135
Utilitarian items, 14, 18

Van der Leeuw, Sander, 32, 138, 139
Venison, 82
Villages, 31

Wall trench, 43, 44, 56
Walthall, John, 28, 29, 173
Wealth, 18
Webb, William S., 52, 166, 167, 185, 187, 195
Welch, Paul, 40, 58, 75, 77, 111, 123, 171, 183, 184

West Jefferson phase, 32, 45, 150–52
Whalen, Michael, 57
White, James F., 36, 42
White site, dates, 52–55; description, 38, 41–42, 51, 70–72; excavations by AMNH, 36–37; excavations by Moore, 34–36; excavations by UMMA, 38–45; location, 34
Williams, Mark, 199
Wimberly, Steve, 28, 184
Women, nonlocal, 172, 175
Wood, 110, 111, 135, 170
Workshop, 124
Works Progress Administration (WPA), 28
Wright, Henry, 1, 7, 15, 16, 20, 177, 191

Yarborough site, 81, 82, 84, 88–93, 96–99, 133
Yarnell, Richard, 115
Yaupon holly *(Ilex vomitoria),* 113–14
Yerkes, Richard, 149

About the Author

Paul D. Welch is Assistant Professor of Anthropology, Queens College, City University of New York. He received a bachelor's degree from Oberlin College and his master's and doctorate from the University of Michigan.